Milton's Vision

Milton's Vision

The Birth of Christian Liberty

Theo Hobson

continuum

Continuum International Publishing Group
The Tower Building   80 Maiden Lane
11 York Road   Suite 704
London   New York
SE1 7NX   NY 10038

www.continuumbooks.com

First published 2008

British Library Cataloguing-in-Publication Data
A catalogue record for this book is available from the British Library.

ISBN 9781847063427

Typeset by Newgen Imaging Systems Pvt Ltd, Chennai, India
Printed and bound by MPG Books, Cornwall

To
Mum and Dad,
and
Norman Bishop,
my grandfather-in-law

Contents

Acknowledgements

I am grateful to those who have encouraged me in this project, including Diarmaid MacCulloch, A. N. Wilson, Caroline Dawnay, George Pattison, John Venning, who reminded me the fourth centenary was coming up, Robin Baird-Smith of Continuum, who has allowed this author to 'be a Doctor in his book as he ought to be' – and above all as ever my wife Tess Wicksteed.

Introduction

If only Milton were alive now: he is exactly what we need. He would cut through all the stagnant clichés about national identity, and the place of religion in society, and offer us a serious, ambitious and essentially simple vision.

My approach to Milton is rather eccentric, in that it takes his religious thought very seriously indeed. This book discusses the poetry, but primarily treats him as a great religious and political thinker – as a genuinely important resource for our time (I dare be known to think him a better teacher than Luther or Calvin). In fact, I believe that his greatness as a poet has obscured this vision. His real potential usefulness to us is in danger of being Paradise-lost.

My claim is that Milton is a crucial resource for understanding the relationship between secular liberalism and religion in the West, particularly Britain and America. He can help to explode the assumption that these two things are opposed. In the liberal Protestant tradition that he helped to launch, secular liberalism and Christianity are allies rather than enemies. They need each other. I believe that this tradition cries out for renewal.

I am not quite claiming that he invented liberal Protestantism. For, before Milton, Protestantism already had a liberal wing, of sorts. Certain late-sixteenth-century reformers talked up toleration (which was not a major concern of the first Protestant reformers). And England's reformation had a sort of liberalism, despite its royalist-episcopal structure. But it was only in Milton's lifetime that this vague tradition really took off. In the first half of the seventeenth-century a more ambitious form of political liberalism emerged – and it emerged together with reformed Christianity; it began to seem, to some, that liberty and Protestantism were not just allies but *the same cause*. No one said so with greater urgency than Milton. He saw that the liberal state is the necessary setting for Protestant Christianity – here alone can it be itself.

To herald Milton as a great thinker feels terrifically unfashionable. Of course his greatness is universally acknowledged, but that is for his poetry. And, when one looks a little closer at his literary reputation, it is evident that no writer is so grudgingly admired. He wrote great poetry, goes the received wisdom, but his creed was narrow, chilling, inhuman. He was a Puritan. This toxic label implies that he supported an authoritarian form of Protestantism that was intent on imposing itself on the nation, banning its fun, policing its very thoughts.

Generations of critics have found it strange, and a bit disturbing, that such a great artist should have been so ideologically involved. For an artist to be politically engaged is all very well, but to become the evangelist for a religious-political cause . . . It will not really do. He went too far. For example one of his most influential twentieth-century biographers, E. M. W. Tillyard, is on the one hand approving: 'Like other great artists he could not afford to cut himself off from the main sources of the mental activity of his age. It was as necessary for Milton to be interested in the Episcopacy as for Homer to be interested in battles, or Virgil in Roman Imperialism.'[1] But just a page later he tells us that an artist is meant to maintain a certain detachment: Milton's religious enthusiasm was 'a defect of character. A man of more capacious mind and a better knowledge of human nature would have known that the premises on which Milton argued were false, that no revolution could change men's hearts in the way Milton imagined . . . A Shakespeare would have had the sense to keep out of active controversy.'[2] This judgement is one of the key orthodoxies of the tradition known as English Literature. Its founder is Samuel Johnson, who loved *Paradise Lost* but saw Milton's politics as unforgivable (rather as we might today see those of Heidegger, the Nazi-friendly

1 E. M. W. Tillyard, *Milton*, London: Penguin (1930), 1968, p. 95.
2 Ibid., p. 96.

philosopher). Some of the Romantics half-challenged it. Blake applauded Milton the revolutionary, and so did Shelley. But their praise muddied the waters by associating Milton with the secular revolutionary spirit of the early nineteenth century. (Blake's claim that Milton was of the devil's party without knowing it is the silliest thing in the history of criticism.) Wordsworth muddied things in a different way, by heralding the archetypal 'prophet', but rooting this in some vague stuff about 'imagination', and failing to engage with his actual thought. In effect, Johnson's verdict was confirmed: the critical consensus separated Milton the poet (good) from Milton the thinker (dangerous, or just deluded). In the twentieth century, the tradition of Tory disdain for Milton's thought was renewed by T. S. Eliot, and a secularist attack also emerged, an aversion to his Christianity. William Empson's literary atheism has been echoed by endless recent writers, who use Milton criticism as a way of displaying their brave rejection of religion. (C. S. Lewis is right: 'Many of those who say they dislike Milton's God only mean that they dislike God.'[3]) The best recent Milton criticism has gone some way to dispelling this trend: critics such as Stanley Fish have shown how theologically naive, and hermeneutically dim, it is to criticize the authoritarianism of the God of *Paradise Lost*. Yet the old cliché still dominates the popular view of Milton: he was a great artist, constrained by a backward ideology, a gloomy bossy mind-myth. Of course feminist criticism has some strident things to add here. (It might as well be admitted straight away that feminism was a blind spot for Milton, as it was for just about every other man of the seventeenth century).

Milton must not be left to the literary critics, with their inherited sneer towards his thought, their lack of interest in theology, and their failure to see his mounting relevance. But who else shows any interest in him? Political historians show some – and recently the Prime Minister, Gordon Brown, name-checked him in a speech on the British tradition of liberty. But, alas, theologians show no interest in him. I consider this a colossal oversight. In my view, his approach to Christianity holds the key to its contemporary renewal.

---

3   C. S. Lewis, *A Preface to Paradise Lost*, London: Oxford University Press, 1960, p. 130.

Some will agree that his ideas were influential, in the Commonwealth period, and then in the Whig movement that formed our liberal constitution, and also in the American Revolution. But those struggles are over, they will say. In A. N. Wilson's words, 'the causes about which he minded so passionately are dead.'[4] Is he not the sort of quintessentially modern thinker who has little to offer postmodernity? Surely the liberal Protestant spirit of the seventeenth century is now a distant thing? Does anyone still care whether the Church of England has bishops, or is established?

I suggest that Milton's liberal Protestantism has become more relevant over the past decade. For we have been rudely awakened to the need to define ourselves, to untangle our liberal, secular and Christian roots. We need to ask how our tradition of liberty arose, in order to see how it works, and how it may be renewed. Should the liberal state be a sort of neutral space in which all ideologies are treated equally? Or should liberalism be more of a positive ideology? To tackle these questions properly we need to go back further than Orwell, or even J. S. Mill. We need to go back to the Reformation and its aftermath: we need to know the difference between Luther and Calvin, we need to know about Henry VIII's weird revolution, that enabled, by tyrannical means, the gradual emergence of a half-liberal state, and we need to know about the affinity between royal absolutism and Roman Catholicism, and the split between conservative and liberal Puritanism, and Cromwell, and the Quakers, and tithes – and Milton.

Those of us who are Christian have an added concern: how is the faith to be renewed in the context of secular liberalism? Is it possible? Milton says yes. He says that authentic Christian faith will always take the liberty-loving path, even if this means the demise of strong religious institutions. Indeed we have to take leave of the concept of institutional orthodoxy if we are to renew Christianity in a politically enlightened age. If the Gospel is to thrive, it must be deregulated. Strange to say, this is still a radical theological idea, three hundred and fifty years on. Are these causes – the renewal of liberalism, and the renewal of Protestantism – dead? Over my dead body.

---

4   A. N. Wilson, *The Life of John Milton*, London: Pimlico (1982), 2002, p. 98.

His greatness is not just about politics and religion; it is also about art. I do not just mean that he was a great poet. I also mean that he was one of the very few great writers to have put art in its place. He is free from the quasi-religious aestheticism that infected literature in the Romantic period, and infects it still. Today's sassy contemporary literary critics will smirk ironically at the idea that their view of literature remains quasi-religious, but it does. What Milton knew, and secular lit-crit cannot, is that beauty is a dangerous thing unless rooted in a wider narrative about goodness and truth.

His greatness is not just about politics, religion and art; it is also about sex. Here the critical smirks will multiply: what can this frigid prude tell us about sex? His work raises crucial questions about the representation of sex. Is it possible to warn against sexual promiscuity, and to celebrate chastity, without being the most awful sort of meddling prude? Is it possible to acknowledge the need for freedom of sexual expression – and also to promote the ideal of resisting temptation? As a young writer he dared to be known as an advocate of chastity – but he was not Mary Whitehouse in a ruff. He wanted to represent the sexiness of sex in order to help people to reflect on the need to resist it. Later on he argued against the banning of erotic literature, on the grounds that grown-up moral agents had to confront the power of sexual desire. Later still he wrote a highly erotic account of Adam and Eve in the Garden of Eden. Part of the point of literature is to help us confront the reality of sex, which is simultaneously thrilling and dangerous. And the same goes for evil. It might sound like a bizarre comparison, but I think there is analogy with Nabokov, especially his most famous novel *Lolita*. It is shocking not just in its subject matter (paedophilia), but even more so in the fact that it makes the paedophile narrator so attractive, such stylish fun to read. Is this immoral, to make a paedophile seem so cool? Or is it in fact very moral indeed, to warn the reader against the potential attractiveness of evil?

A brief word about the structure of what follows. Because I want to focus on his religious thought, I feel it necessary to start with an account of the Reformation. In particular, I want to show how Protestantism is still in the process of formation when Milton starts thinking; its relationship to the emergent liberal movement remains completely unfixed. This provision of background might seem like trying the patience of readers who want to read about Milton, but as they will eventually find out, patience is a very Miltonic virtue.

1

The Broken Revolution

Milton was born into a revolution, a long revolution. For the past eighty or ninety years Europe had been in turmoil, due to a strange mutation of its religion that spread through most of its northern half. This mutation refused to stabilize: the meaning of Protestantism was unsettled. It was certainly a revolution, but what sort of revolution? What was its political agenda? What was its relationship to the liberal humanism of the Renaissance? What *was* this new ideology?

These questions remained, in many respects, wide open. This is the key to understanding Milton's greatness: he helped to define a version of Protestantism, a version that would have huge influence on subsequent centuries. In order to understand how he did this, we must give an account of the Reformation so far, showing how this revolution remained open, unsettled, broken.

Our central theme is the relationship between Protestantism and freedom. But this story has a prologue, called the Renaissance. In the early fourteenth century, an intellectual and artistic renaissance was already well underway in Northern Italy. It was rooted in a new political attitude of the city-states. Cities such as Padua and Florence were proud of their effective independence from the Holy Roman Empire. They trumpeted their 'liberty', and appealed to the Roman Republic as a model. The new intellectuals, the humanists, revived of the idea of classical 'virtue', which meant above all political pride. They were dismissive of the 'scholastic' theology of Aquinas, which seemed full of irrelevant abstraction. Their study of classical literature led to a huge interest in rhetoric, a practical, politically engaged form of discourse. Also, of course it led to a more positive and excited attitude to secular life. The success of one's city was something to celebrate – on the classical model. Such celebration was theologically questionable. To affirm wealth, and military strength implied a strong criticism of medieval piety, gloomy otherworldliness (Machiavelli was the culmination of this Renaissance trend). The new arts of vernacular poetry and painting gradually became more neo-pagan. Dante's dabbling in classical myth had been restrained; his followers Petrarch and Boccaccio were less careful. Painting followed suit, though more slowly: the pious restraint of Giotto gradually yielded to the lush flesh of Botticelli. Intellectuals became bolder in proclaiming that the 'dark ages' were being overcome by 'enlightenment', and the 'rebirth' of culture. Such imagery verges on blasphemy, in its location of light and life in the classical world rather than in Christian revelation.

Humanism had a carefully a muted anti-papal wing. For Marsiglio of Padua, the new mood of civic liberty entailed freedom from a politically ambitious papacy. He argued that the Church had no legitimate secular power. This idea quietly spread through the humanist class, but was seldom voiced. It was voiced, however, by the Oxford theologian John Wycliffe in the late fourteenth century. He taught that the papacy was a fallible human institution that ought to be subservient to the Gospel, as known through scripture. He also argued that the reform of the Church fell to the king, for the Church's corruption was rooted in its wealth, which it was not likely to surrender voluntarily. His thought briefly found favour at court. It happened that England was linked to Bohemia, in eastern Europe, by royal marriage. Bohemian courtiers brought back Wycliffe's writings and they helped to inspire John Hus's reform movement. Hus was condemned by a papal council and burned as a heretic in 1415. But Rome's tough tactics were counter-productive: the people of Bohemia rose in revolt against Rome, and secured independence for their Church.

But the Bohemian experience was exceptional. The humanist consensus was that the Church should be reformed, not rejected; that a reformed Church was essential to the health of Christendom. Humanism saw itself as the critical friend of the Church. But in practice it was a threat – partly because it encouraged princes to see themselves in the mirror of classical history, but also because it was interested in re-thinking Christianity – by analyzing its founding texts, and by asking existential questions about the real meaning of faith.

Why didn't humanism turn into a full-scale attack on the Church? Because such rebellion was also political rebellion, and associated with dangerous fanatics. The humanist, by contrast, idealized order, civilization. It might even be said that an outright rejection of the Church was, to the humanist, *literally* unthinkable. It would take a new sort of style, a new sort of rhetorical performance. It would take a radical departure from the politic style of humanist discourse. It was unthinkable even to Erasmus, who was passionately committed to religious reform. He wanted to re-root theology in the exegesis of the New Testament. He massively contributed to biblical scholarship by producing an edition of the New Testament in its original Greek, in 1516. His cause was religious and secular education, open to all: he imagined a new, proud form of culture in which the boy at the plough would recite scripture as he worked. He was the prototype of the modern liberal theologian, who seeks a more reasonable account of Christianity's truth. He believed in one great tradition of wisdom, in which Socrates and Jesus were colleagues. He hoped that the Church would become more reasonable, more open-minded, a force for 'concordia', world peace.

But this reformer did not quite have teeth. Any real transformation of Christendom had to come from a positive harnessing of this religion, in all its fiery intensity. Change would not come from a plea for reasonability but from a prophetic demand for God's truth.

Luther

Luther, more than anyone else, invented the modern pathos of a revolutionary commitment to truth, and to its promise of liberation. 'The truth shall set you free': this became, through him, the motto of modernity. He taught modern Christianity its passionate and revolutionary attachment to freedom.

He was a monk-academic at a new university in Saxony. His big idea (that he found in Augustine) was that salvation is not the result of any human effort but the gift of God. Instead of trying very hard to be holy, one had to trust in God, let him take control. The Church had to abandon its bad old theology of 'works' – and its interest in secular power. But it showed no signs of doing so. It was actually reviving the huge con of indulgences, written assurances of the remission of sin. The idea was that the saints had got to heaven so easily that they had created a surplus of salvation, a 'treasury of merit' that the Church could tap, to help others move more quickly through purgatory towards salvation. The scheme had begun as a form of emergency fund-raising for the Crusades; it was now raising funds for extravagant buildings in Rome (including the dome of St Peter's). When a new sales-drive hit Germany in 1517, Luther spoke out.

Even back then, the public tended to ignore rants from theologians. But his protest chimed in with a new political shift: some German humanists were arguing that Rome's power stood in the way of national identity. Germany was the largest region of the Holy Roman Empire. It was ruled by various princes and dukes, all subject to the Emperor. This was unsatisfactory: as the largest part of the Empire by far, Germany ought to have been supreme in Europe, but instead it felt hard done by. The resentment was increasingly focused on the role of the Church: why should Germany be subject to Italian power and pay taxes to Rome?

Luther believed, with touching naivety, that the Church would see his point, and put an end to the abuse. Of course he was told that the authority of the Church had to be respected: away from this principle lay chaos, and hydra-headed heresy. What enabled Luther to resist the force of this argument was his sympathy with the mystical, apocalyptic idea that the Church would, in the last days of history, be possessed by the Devil, provoking the Second Coming. Before 1517 this picture lurked at the back of his mind. Now it came to the front. If the papacy blocked the reform that all good Christians yearned for, in what sense was it *not* the tool of the Antichrist?

Erasmus had insisted that the Church must reform itself. Luther was taking this a step further: if it does not move in the direction of reform, it is not the true Church. But, of course this next step is a leap of faith, a leap into the theological unknown. It meant rejecting the Church as a strong, united, autonomous institution, as a *reality*. His ecclesiological purism is from one perspective very close to ecclesiological nihilism. To call for a Church without worldly power is utopian. It means rejecting what is flawed, but does at least exist, for the sake of an idea. How would a new pure Church come into being? God knew. This faith-based *recklessness* is the real key to Luther. His belief in the Last Days is a crucial factor, and it puts him in the company of Paul, who was similarly willing to leave questions of religious organization to God.

He became one of the first media figures: pamphlets dramatized his rebellion and cartoons hailed him as the German Hercules. He found that he rather liked being a celebrity. When Rome condemned him for heresy in 1520 he publicly burned the bull (the papal document) condemning him; a classic woodcut-opportunity. And his full-scale polemical writing began, with the publication of some astonishing tracts. He attacked the assumption that the world is divided into a religious and a secular class: all Christians belong to the religious class. A priest is not a higher sort of Christian, just a job. And he called on Germany's secular rulers to take religious responsibility for the spiritual welfare of their people. They must reject canon law, which is harmful as well as false (he explains that the ban on priestly marriage leads to sexual abuse). Luther's rhetoric is full of realism: we must pull down the illusion that there is a middle-entity, the Roman Church, between what is worldly and what is spiritual.

Following Paul, he rejects the idea of a holy law. This is really the essence of his Protestantism: that no religious institution should lay down the law in God's name. For the good news of the Gospel is that God's grace is not dependent on us following the moral or cultic rules. This is not to do away with morality or law, but to shift them to the secular sphere. If morality is not prescribed in a divine law, there must be a new respect for secular law. This is basically the origin of modern secularism. The only valid law is the secular law, which is indirectly divinely ordained (God tells us to obey the secular ruler). It follows that no religious institution can claim to override the state's legal authority.

Luther's secularizing effect must be understood in connection with his elevation of rhetoric. What replaces the authority of the Roman Church is not the Bible, but a certain form of speech (and writing – and thought, and feeling) rooted in the Bible. Of course it is Paul's voice above all, that is re-performed, expanded upon. Christianity is participation in Pauline rhetoric, in the speech-act whereby grace is preferred to the law. Luther's sermons are full of dramatic rhetorical combat with Satan.

In 1521, he refused to recant at the Diet of Worms. It remains the greatest prophetic impersonation in modern religious history. The Emperor Charles duly issued a condemnation of him, but he was tentatively supported by his local prince, Frederick: he spent almost a year in one of his castles, directing Wittenberg's reform from afar, and translating some of the Bible into German. He still hoped that all the German princes would back his revolution, but things actually started moving in a more grassroots way. Questions naturally arose about what reform ought to mean. A reformed church did not take shape naturally, like a body regaining its proper posture when released from constricting chains. A new model had to be invented. Luther insisted that this was the princes' task: it was for them to supply the order that this movement needed; else it would collapse into chaos. Everything depended on the secular ruler's involvement. This is the basis of the position known as 'magisterial' (meaning that it involves the secular ruler, or magistrate).

But some took another view. When he returned to Wittenberg he found that his authority was challenged by a clique of radicals, who said that the true church should not collude with political power, that it should be a sect, a counter-culture. They questioned the practice of infant baptism; church membership required a conscious adult decision of faith. Luther was violently opposed to these people, whom he called fanatics, madmen. They were erecting a new law, for a church that was a counter-cultural sect would surround 'authentic Christianity' with tight rules about morality and ritual. Luther saw that such legalism could only be avoided if the state stepped in to direct reform. His repeated point was that the new religious order must be directed by the secular ruler. Because religion is part of public life, it must follow rules, but such rules are external to religion itself. For example, if some sect wants to parade around naked for the sake of the Gospel, they must be stopped on *political* grounds. To prohibit them on religious grounds would be to turn the Gospel into law; to make clothes-wearing a sacred matter.

Surprising as it may sound, Luther did not want to lay down a blueprint for reformed worship. Of course he called for the removal of explicit papalism from the service, but when an issue was ambiguous he was carefully conservative. He often repeated the dictum: 'We must not turn freedom into law.'[1] In other words, we must not insist on doing something in a new, 'pure' way that then becomes mandatory. In terms of worship there could be no simple 'back to basics' movement: the attempt to base one's practice strictly on the New Testament was dangerous (infant baptism would have to go).

He saw Christianity as a sort of religious anarchism that needed the state to protect it. He did not believe in the church as an autonomous institution. In 1524 a fellow reformer suggested that differences in reformed practice should be settled by an evangelical council. Luther rejected the idea, insisting that local diversity was healthy.[2] He trusted in God's ownership of this revolution. It is an incredibly naïve ecclesiology: let it be, God is in control. The true church will simply emerge, as the good news of the Gospel spreads – there is no need for central planning (except what the prince deems necessary for order). The only authentic 'body' is the state, and the church finds partial embodiment, thanks to the state. So Lutheran Protestantism entails a half-turn away from the very concept of church. An autonomous institutional church has become illegitimate; the church ought to be a department of state.

This is what began to happen. Later in 1524 religious radicals prodded the peasants of Germany to revolt. Luther repeated his support for the forces of law and order, in notoriously violent terms. This hard line paid off, winning him credibility with the German princes – the first ones now came out in direct support, making their territory officially Lutheran.

---

1   Luther, quoted in Heinrich Bornkamm, *Luther in Mid-Career 1521–30*, Philadelphia: Fortress Press, 1983, p. 136.
2   Ibid., p. 470.

Zwingli

We must be wary of the term 'the Reformation', for it implies that the differences between the reformers are negligible, inessential. This is not the case. (We must be similarly wary of 'Protestantism' of course.)

The other really influential form of reformation began in Zurich, a small but particularly proud example of the city-state. The proud, strong Council saw itself as a Christian body. It did not need a foreign bishop to direct it. On the other hand, this unitive model was incomplete: the city accepted that doctrinal and liturgical matters were the business of Rome; it accepted the hierarchy as the external arbiter of orthodoxy.

Under Zwingli, the city took full control of its religious life; it became, in a sense, its own church. It is this involvement of the city council that distinguishes what becomes known as the 'Reformed' tradition from the Lutheran. In the city-state model the gap between religion and politics melts away, for Christian citizens participate in political life. For Luther, by contrast, worldly power remains distant, other. It is exercised by a special breed, called Princes. They are rather exotic beasts, necessarily fearsome: ermined lions. The Christian can only hope that God will in his mercy provide us with good lions, whose violence serves the cause of the Gospel.

It would seem that the city-state model of reform is therefore more progressive, more modern, for something resembling democracy is at work. But as we shall see, things are less simple. The intimate relationship between political power and the reformist cause is in practice not so benign; it is less willing to leave theological questions open.

From around 1516, Huldrych Zwingli, a priest and humanist, started developing a sort of semi-utopian vision, of the perfect Christian society emerging once the Church was purged of clerical worldliness. There would be a perfect integration of the religious and the political. The model was Israel. Zurich felt called to show the world a Christian Israel, a 'covenant people'.

Zwingli began persuading Zurich's Council to take full charge of the city's religious practice. He told it that it was possessed of intrinsic religious authority, for according to the Bible authority lay with the local assembly of Christians – which should be interpreted to mean all of

Zurich. In effect he was saying that the Council was not only a secular body but also a religious one; the local expression of the universal church. The polis was a religious as well as a political entity – just like Israel. As in Israel, there should still be a religious sphere, run by priests, but it should not be answerable to a foreign hierarchy, but only to the polis. It was a new vision of religious and political unity.

So the Council set about reforming worship; above all abolishing the idolatry of the Mass. But, as in Wittenberg, progress was threatened by the impatience of a radical party, who could not wait for a slow, bureaucratic reform. Zwingli continued to assert that order came first. Like Luther, he had to show that the reformist cause was no anarchism. Where he differs from Luther is in his idealistic conviction that magistrate and priest can complement each other to create total religious harmony: 'when the Gospel is preached and all, including the magistrate, heed it, the Christian man is nothing else than the faithful and good citizen; and the Christian city is nothing other than the Christian Church.'[3] Luther would have suspected such rhetoric of utopianism.

Zwingli was careful to keep the reform movement moving slowly, so that the politicians would not be scared by its anarchic wing, but would gradually assume ownership of it. He waited a few years before openly expressing his sexuality, coming out – as a married man. Priestly marriage was seen as shocking. Marriage became a staple gesture for the reformer; a rebuke to the centuries-old prejudice that a really holy man would be celibate. (Luther's marriage to an ex-nun served to underline the point twice.) Manliness was also displayed by means of long beards.

Worship was reformed according to scripture, or rather Zwingli's interpretation of scripture. A purist minimalism was imposed; music was considered a sort of invisible idolatry and so the organs were ripped from churches. The Eucharist was reinvented in an almost rationalist way: it was the pledge of the congregation's allegiance; nothing magical happened.

---

3   Zwingli, *On Divine and Human Righteousness*, Works XIV, 424, 12–22, quoted in Robert C. Walton, *Zwingli's Theocracy*, Toronto: University of Toronto Press, 1967, p. 169.

The radical sectarian reformers became defined by their approach to baptism. Infant baptism was unbiblical, they complained, and so acquired their name 'Anabaptists', meaning 're-baptisers'. They were right that infant baptism had no warrant in the New Testament, so how did Zwingli justify it? It should be seen as the Christian version of circumcision, he said: the sign of God's covenant with his people. It was another pledge of group identity. The sacraments were holy because they defined this community as the new Israel. Luther lacked this consistent desire to imagine the reformed community as the new Israel.

Zwingli's difference from Luther is that he felt himself to be *of* the secular authority – indeed, as a citizen of a city-state, he was. A related point is simply one of scale. Luther saw Wittenberg as a small part of Saxony, which was in turn a small part of the Empire. His conservatism was partly strategic. If reform was to spread throughout the Empire, it would have to seem an attractive proposition to the princes. Zwingli lacked this concern: Zurich was a world in itself. The way forward was to create a godly city that others would imitate. The different political contexts of Wittenberg and Zurich create the hugest theological difference. Luther demands a new *separation* of religion and politics: the Gospel must be purged of worldly power, authoritarianism, legalism; which means that the state must step in to order its dissemination. Zwingli demands a new *unity* of religion and politics, on Israelite lines. Once the worldly religion of Rome is removed, a new sort of Christian polity becomes possible. The danger of a total religious society is obvious.

Relations between the two reformations were frosty. Yet by the late 1520s the secular masters of each reformation formed an alliance. At the imperial Diet of Speyer in 1529 they united in a 'Protestation' against the empire's official Catholic policy – and 'Protestantism' was born. It's worth underlining that 'Protestantism' was a loose coalition invented by politicians – it has not really gained in coherence since.

The new political alliance of the Protestants provoked an aggressive Catholic reaction: Zurich was attacked, and Zwingli himself was killed in the battle. Luther lived on until 1546, writing potent propaganda for his Protestant princes. The anarchic streak within his theology was reined in by the need to create stable new state churches, and toughen them against Rome. Such churches began to emerge in Germany and Scandinavia, and a mutant version had reshaped England, under an ego to rival his.

Henry

England was the most complex and fruitful site of Protestantism's political development. Here, as nowhere else, national idealism, and royal power, entered the equation.

Henry VIII was an ambitious young Renaissance prince. He turned the court into an endless spectacle, starring him. He also fancied himself as a good Catholic – for a while. He suppressed Lutheran literature, and renewed the ban on translating the Bible into English. But he had learned from his humanist teachers that the Church needed reforming, that it was hopelessly embroiled in worldly politics. And he was quick to agree: he saw the power and grandeur of the Church as competition. On the other hand, he could not rule without the Church. Secular and religious government were probably more closely united in England than anywhere else in western Christendom. His chief minister, Cardinal Wolsey, was also the Pope's legate.

Luther's message caused English ripples. William Tyndale went into exile to translate the Bible: by 1526 the first copies were circulating in England, and creating a new mood of evangelical confidence. It is worth underlining that a vernacular Bible combines Protestantism with two big forces: national pride, and enlightenment. A movement that promotes English as the proper language of God, at least for the English, can hardly be called unpatriotic. With the translation of scripture, the rhetoric of religious truth became available to the layman in a new way. One could echo the rhetoric of Jesus and Paul. And the translation of the Bible meant that reformers were intrinsically 'humanists', friends of learning, and press freedom. So English Protestantism begins with this enviably strong narrative: it is pro-English, pro-enlightenment, and pro-freedom. And the translation of the Bible highlights this like nothing else.

Henry's chief religious adviser was Thomas More: a conservative humanist. Luther's revolution led only to chaos, he told his master: persecution was a duty. More embodies the limits of Catholic humanism: he had to choose between his love of free inquiry and his loyalty to Rome.

Henry's wife was failing to bear him a male heir, which made him feel insecure. Was it because she was his late brother's widow, and the marriage was cursed? In 1526 he fell in love with a new face at court, a provocatively self-confident beauty, sexily unfazed by Henry. Anne Boleyn was the daughter of Thomas Boleyn, a leading patron of England's tentative reformers. There was a national dimension to her allure: this feisty independent-minded English girl was a stark contrast to his foreign wife, who now retreated further into her foreignness, and her Catholic piety. Henry began to mythologise Anne; she signified a new future for England, an ideal of national independence. And Catherine, being Spanish, began to symbolize England's servitude to foreign power.

When the Pope refused to declare his marriage invalid, he began breaking with Rome. But this questioning of papal authority did not put him in Luther's camp. He did not even move one foot into that camp. His theological outlook remained essentially Erasmian – with a dash of Machiavelli of course. The only evidence that he had any sympathy at all with Lutheranism is that Anne was sympathetic, but he probably saw her sympathy as endearingly naive. The new theology, he would have gently explained to her, was a threat to national security – that's why his nice ministers were repressing it. On the other hand, he was obviously aware of the new powers that Lutheranism offered secular rulers.

Outwardly he was still a Catholic monarch, persecuting Lutheranism (by means of his Lord Chancellor Thomas More, who ordered thirty burnings) – yet he now appointed Cranmer Archbishop of Canterbury. And then the mask of papal loyalty was removed, once Anne was pregnant, and the 'Reformation Parliament' began to pass the legislation that broke with Rome. The Act in Restraint of Appeals contained the clearest justification so far for the break with Rome: 'This realm of England is an empire . . . governed by one supreme head and king', it announced: there was no place for papal rule. The Act presented itself as a restoration of the monarch's rights.

The English Church was now severed from papal authority. But where did that put it? There was still no declaration in favour of Lutheranism; churchmen were expected to be religious conservatives. Henry did not really have a religious policy, beyond demanding that the clergy were obedient to him rather than the Pope. He had no desire to import Lutheran theology: why should a dodgy German become an authority in England? This aversion to Lutheranism is ironic: Henry was quietly setting the English reformation on an ultra-Lutheran course, in its absolute magisterialism and in its conservatism regarding worship.

So the English Reformation, in its first phase, pretended that it wasn't happening – despite the revolution of the dissolution of the monasteries. This had nothing to do with theology, in the official account; it simply restored the monarch's right to his own land. The English Church served no theological system, except 'tradition', 'orthodoxy'; it served the nation. Henry was not pursuing a compromise, designing the Anglican 'third way'. He actually believed that the English Church had now been fully and finally reformed, by virtue of being nationalised.

Cranmer gave full theological backing to the principle of royal supremacy in the Church. God intended princes to have total control over religious as well as civil government. This perhaps even goes beyond the magisterialism of Luther. As Cranmer's biographer says, 'he revealed a breathtaking scepticism about any independent character for the church.'[4] He realized that Henry's approach was actually very effective in welding church and state together, and setting both on a slow but sure reforming course. The way to reform the English Church was slowly-slowly. England could not be treated like a very big Swiss city-state. Its scale meant that the preservation of unity under the crown must be put before the pursuit of theological purity.

Henry's reformation was not so much 'Protestant' as secular. The aim was the removal of a religious form of authority that inhibited the exercise of secular power. We are inclined to assume that a religious thing called the Reformation had secular consequences. In the English context,

---

4   Diarmaid MacCulloch, *Reformation: Europe's House Divided 1490–1700*, London: Penguin 2003, p. 278.

this is the wrong way round: a secularist revolution, the removal of papal authority, enabled the gradual rise of new religious thought.

And this reformation enabled a uniquely open form of Protestantism. Because Henry allowed no new theological orthodoxy to take root, he forced reformed thought into an uncomfortable but fruitful posture of openness. Consequently this form of Protestantism inhaled the air of humanism more deeply than any other. Henry was a providential egomaniac.

Calvin

France's religious situation in the late 1520s was in many ways similar to England's. The king, Francis I, became increasingly besieged by a reformist faction, which included the young humanist lawyer John Calvin. At first he was a fringe member, more interested in establishing himself as a classical scholar. Compared to Luther, his zeal was cool, careful, considered. He seems to have suspected both Luther and Zwingli of irreverence, of neglecting priestly order, hieratic propriety. The ceremonial majesty of the Church should not be rejected, he felt, but better founded – in flawless doctrine. He was even more conscious than Luther and Zwingli of the danger of sectarianism – for the Reformation had shown itself to be vulnerable to disorder. Compared to Luther, Calvin never made a full psychological break with the old Church: he wanted a new, pure version of Roman Catholicism.

In 1534, he fled to Basel, where he sharpened his thought, and gained standing among the reformers. In 1536 he published the first edition of his big book, *The Institutes of Christianity* ('The Institutes' meaning 'the basics'). It was dedicated to Francis, his king. The prefatory letter explains that the reformist cause is not a dangerous revolution but a restoration of true godly order. This claim to be on the side of God's orderly power is the key function of Calvin's prose. His grandly authoritative style attempts to stand in for the actual authority of the institution of the Church, currently almost completely absent. (This, to anticipate, is an area of overlap with Milton.)

His book smells of order; it is dauntingly large and intricate, like a new machine. And of course its theme is order, the order of God. All goodness, truth and order reside in God, not in us. Of course this follows Luther's basic insistence that we are sinners absolutely dependent on God's grace. But Calvin expounds this in a new key. There is a quasi-rational approach; a sort of literal-mindedness. Luther's writing is poetic, extravagant, theatrical: he is constantly cursing the Devil, and off on rhetorical flights. There is none of this in Calvin. His *Institutes* is more like a science text-book, telling us exactly what we need to know.

Most of what we need to know is our own depravity, which Calvin expounds with psychological care. There is a new emphasis on individual salvation or damnation in the afterlife. In Luther's work this territory remains vague; his emphasis is on our salvation *now*, as we receive and re-issue the Word, as we are taken up by its tsunami-like force.

But what really distinguishes Calvin from Luther is his belief in the church. We noted that Luther simply did not believe in the church as an autonomous, authoritative institution. Calvin simply did. And, just after the *Institutes*' publication, he was invited to put this belief into practice. The Genevan church asked for his help. The city, recently independent, was in need of leadership. It lacked a strong ruling class, and the town council looked to the church to fill the void. When Calvin requested new powers for the church, making it effectively the city's executive authority, they were granted. The council authorized the creation of a parallel body, the consistory. As well as priests and deacons this body contained lay elders. It was a strong, largely democratic body that eclipsed the secular council. It had the power to excommunicate offenders, so as to preserve the church's purity. It required the city council to do the dirty work of punishing these offenders, even banishing them from the city, or even occasionally executing them.

So the Church is an institution in the world that exercises authority. Like a Roman Catholic, he insists that 'the keys have been given to the Church': it is empowered to excommunicate the ungodly, to mediate divine judgement.[5] The church mediates God's law. He repeatedly emphasizes that the moral content of the law is not revoked by Christ (as opposed to the ceremonial and judicial elements, which are). He preached

5   Calvin, *Institutes of the Christian Religion*, trans. by Henry Beveridge, Michigan: Eerdmans, 1989, 3.I, p. 298.

endless sermons on the Decalogue, the Ten Commandments. Though salvation is by grace, we must keep obeying God's law as far as we are able. And the religious and secular authorities must combine to promote this law.

In the 1540s, Calvin's church began to implement a sort of cultural revolution. The city had to become a beacon of moral order, it had to show by its upright habits of life that it had got religion right. Ambitious schemes were hatched, such as a chain of godly pubs, with hymns instead of bawdy songs and dancing (they didn't catch on). Secular entertainments were discouraged: a play about Hercules was banned, for example. The idea was the nurturing of a proudly Christian society.

Calvin was opposed by a few liberal types, but most theologians felt that a hard man was needed, to create an orderly alternative to Rome, attractive to princes. Calvin continued to hope that Geneva would inspire all of France to follow suit. But things didn't look hopeful. In 1539 Francis had reintroduced the Inquisition. He had to be shown that Protestantism could do inquisitions too. Calvin's chance came in 1553, when the errant theologian Miguel Servetus turned up in Geneva. He was a Spanish humanist heretic, who had fled the Spanish Inquisition. In his youth he had imbibed Spain's doomed interfaith culture; he had learned Arabic and Hebrew. He rejected the doctrine of the Trinity, in favour of a sort of mystical rationalism: he believed that a new era had dawned in which God was making himself fully knowable through his creation. The Inquisition pursued him for a decade and finally discovered him working as a doctor in France. He should not have fled to Geneva, for Calvin wanted to show himself to be as tough on heresy as the Roman Church. Calling Servetus' ideas 'poison' he called for his death. The council agreed; he was burned at the stake. Calvin's fame reached new heights, as the tough-guy of Protestantism.

There were some more liberal voices within the Reformed tradition. The year after Servetus' death a Geneva-based theologian, Sebastian Castellio, condemned Calvin's decision. His book *Whether Heretics Should be Persecuted* was an important early call for toleration. Calvin managed to forbid him from teaching: he moved to Basel. Castellio was developing the thought of Guillaume Postel who had written a liberal

the Calvinist style of worship, centred on preaching. She was in many ways a religious conservative, like her father. She had a particular dislike of married priests. She wanted an orderly episcopal Church, fully obedient to her. In a sense she was the first Tory Anglican, allergic to theological enthusiasm of any description. Her famous promise not to 'make windows into men's hearts' was pragmatic: as long as people obeyed her, they could believe what they wanted. Her early policy on Roman Catholic recusancy was remarkably tolerant, to the anger of Parliament. Parliament was now keenly Protestant, and a vocal lobby of MPs wanted to be involved in the running of the Church. She effectively kept power in the hands of herself and a small group of trusted counselors.

Protestant dissatisfaction with her would have grown dangerously strong if it had not been for her role on the international stage. She backed Scotland's Puritan revolution of 1560, and the Calvinist insurgencies in France and the Netherlands. Her anti-Catholic credentials grew stronger in 1569, when the Pope tried to capitalize on a rebellion of Catholic earls by issuing a fatwa condemning her, and encouraging Catholics to resist her. It was a huge own-goal, for now England's religious conservatives were politically suspect, and her religious policy became more reformist.

In 1572, Catholicism showed its true bloody nature, when French Protestants, who had been semi-tolerated for a while, were brutally repressed in the St Bartholomew's Day massacre. The killing in Paris was feverish, mad, Rwandan; a horrible foretaste of the Revolution. The news from France contributed to a sense of English superiority: such medieval barbarism had been left behind, along with loyalty to the Pope. Anglicanism was strengthened by the contrast: it could claim to bring peace, liberty, civilization. In the next decade, this was confirmed by victory over Spain. God seemed to favour this exemplary Protestant, but not too Protestant, nation. Here was the *orderly* alternative to Roman Catholic tyranny.

But Puritanism was getting stronger. Such ideas spread by means of semi-secret preaching-clubs. The bishops were attacked in the Marprelate tracts, an early form of bitterly irreverent journalism. Why was opposition to episcopacy so virulent? Because the idea of an elite with intrinsic spiritual power seemed essentially Catholic rather than Protestant. The Puritans seemed proved right in 1598, when Archbishop Bancroft proclaimed the divine right of episcopacy. In response Robert Browne launched a sect that rejected the Church's compromise. England's powerful non-conformist tradition was underway.

But at the same time the established Church found its supreme apologist: Richard Hooker. During the 1590s, he wrote *The Laws of Ecclesiastical Polity*. It argued that a firmly established church was the best of all possible churches, and enabled the best of all possible states. Hooker showed that an established Church is a relatively liberal one – for religious uniformity becomes a political matter rather than a religious one, and this allows for a high degree of freedom of conscience. It is in the state's interest not to enforce uniformity too rigidly – it can afford to tolerate religious dissent that is discreet rather than proselytizing. As Elton says, the Anglican *via media* was 'the one religious position of the sixteenth century that had within it the germ of toleration.'[8]

In some respects Puritanism was triumphing: there was a steady suppression of folk-religion, public ritual, mystery plays. In Chester for example, mystery plays were last performed in 1574; and processions were gradually tamed – in 1599 the spoil-sport of a mayor banned the inclusion of the traditional 'dragon and naked boys'.[9] Maypoles were felled in many parts of the country. Dramatic spectacle migrated to the tighter confines of London's theatres and above all its court, where royal ritual saw new heights of magnificence.

Elizabeth made England the world centre of art and learning, the new cradle of liberal values. By consolidating a Protestant state, she allowed Protestantism to develop in a new direction: to form a frail alliance with liberty.

She was succeeded by the Scottish king James Stuart in 1603. He had been taught by some austere disciples of Calvin, full of rhetoric about God's judgement on ungodly kings. He learned the opposite lesson: that

---

8   G. R. Elton, *England Under the Tudors*, London: Routledge 1991, p. 427.
9   Patrick Collinson, *The Religion of Protestants, the Church in English Society 1529–1625*, Oxford: Oxford University Press, 1982, p. 226.

such rhetoric was dangerous, that it gave officious men ideas above their station. He developed a strong belief in the divine right of kings. Such a creed is a reaction to Calvinism, whether it is openly revolutionary, or whether it pleads for toleration.

The Puritans hoped that a new ascendancy awaited them, and Catholics hoped for new leniency. James vaguely assured the Puritans that he was on their side, yet he was clear that episcopacy was non-negotiable. His famous pronouncement 'No bishop, no king' is a pithy insistence that the power of the English crown relied upon its episcopal control of the Church. To seek the overthrow of episcopacy was therefore seditious. It raised James' Protestant credentials that he was nearly blown up by Catholic terrorists. But not for very long: it was soon clear that he had no reforming agenda.

2

A Literary Calling

Milton said that a poet should think of his own life as a sort of poem. This sounds like something that might be said much later, by a romantic, or an aesthete. But of course he was very far from being a romantic or an aesthete. He meant that a poet should live in the knowledge that how one lives is one's most basic and powerful form of utterance. Personal morality precedes art. In fact, Milton's suggestion is the antithesis of W. B. Yeats' assertion that one must choose 'perfection of the life or perfection of the work'. The Christian author knows that such a separation makes an idol of art.

His character has been subjected to centuries of sneery criticism: he was proud, priggish, earnest, repressed. One of his biographers, A. L. Rowse, constantly compares him to Shakespeare, in order to highlight his lack of *joie de vivre*, and repeatedly ascribes his coldness to repressed homosexuality.

> William Shakespeare was divinely normal, . . . happily heterosexual . . ., not tormented by religious belief, conventional about all that; . . . a merry, above all an *accepting* nature . . . John Milton was in complete contrast to all this. He could accept nothing on trust: he had to go into everything for himself, satisfying himself intellectually on every point . . . He had nothing of the adorable fluency and flexibility of Shakespeare's nature.[10]

---

10   A. L. Rowse, *Milton the Puritan*, London: Macmillan, 1977, p. 283–4.

Countless others have enjoyed condemning his awkward coldness, and imagining its extension into the bedroom. It is probably true that he was not a great laugh to go drinking with. But we do not have to go drinking with him. We do not even have to read him if we do not want to. It is a tedious pose of bookish critics, to sound so utterly fun-loving that they can hardly bear to contemplate Milton's dourness. He was a serious, introverted type, with a polemical streak, but what is remarkable is that he turned his difficult character to the creation of humane public thought, and public art.

It is natural enough that subsequent writers should resent him. How dare someone believe so firmly in his greatness, and be fully justified? Of course Milton's exceptional arrogance causes resentment in the run-of-the-mill writer, with his run-of-the-mill arrogance. And of course modern literary intellectuals who dislike religion and worship art hate to be told, by a supremely great artist, that art should know its place: in the service of God.

His father, John Milton senior, was somebody in the City, somebody very successful. He was an Oxford graduate, accomplished in music, and in languages. He had fallen out with his own father over religion: the father was a Catholic who repeatedly paid fines for recusancy rather than attend Anglican worship. Without an inheritance to fall back on, Milton's father worked hard to establish himself in the City, and projected his artistic and intellectual interests onto the eldest of his two sons. We know little of Milton's father's religious opinions (and even less of his mother's). What we do know is that he encouraged his son to be a budding humanist, a citizen of the literary world, feeling that no text, ancient or modern, was alien to him. He hired a Scot as his son's tutor – Thomas Young, who would later be an influential Presbyterian theologian. The boy was precociously bookish: he often kept reading till midnight.

From his tutor, and his father, and above all from the culture around him, he imbibed a Protestant pride, tied up with a patriotism that still bore Elizabeth's impression. One of his main guides to recent history was the bestseller of the Elizabethan era: Foxe's *Acts and Monuments*, known as *The Book of Martyrs*. This lively work of propaganda emphasizes the association between reform and enlightenment, and firmly associates

Roman Catholicism with superstition and tyranny. It presents the Reformation as originally English: Wycliffe takes on 'the pernicious superstition of the friars', and the 'ignorance and darkness' and 'extreme tyranny' of the Church. Foxe's account of Luther is stirringly heroic:

> What a miracle this might seem to be, for one man, and a poor friar, creping out of a blind cloister, to be set up against the Pope, the universal bishop, and God's mighty bishop on earth; to withstand all his cardinals, yea, and to sustain the malice and hatred of almost the whole world being set against him; and to work that against the said Pope, cardinals, and Church of Rome, which no king or emperor could ever do, yea, durst ever attempt, nor all the learned men before him could ever compass: which miraculous work of God, I account nothing inferior to the miracle of David overthrowing the great Goliath.[11]

Protestantism is heroic, and dramatic. Foxe offers countless narratives in which stoic Protestants calmly answer their fanatical tormentors. Milton developed a taste for this calm, truth-telling rhetoric – he would later go further than Foxe and write speeches for a rather stoic Christ. And he imbibed Foxe's confidence that England's Protestantism was intrinsically liberal, allergic to persecution (this was not entirely the case, but it could at least claim to be more liberal than Catholicism).

The boy's interest in religion and politics was secondary to his interest in imaginative literature. He was a precocious devotee of classical poetry, finding the mythological excitement in Virgil and Ovid that is nowadays found in Tolkein or Harry Potter. Such excitement was also to be found in recent English writing. His great literary hero, from boyhood on, was Edmund Spenser. Spenser was the most keenly Protestant of the great Elizabethan poets. More than Wyatt, Sidney or Shakespeare, he had wanted to baptize the semi-pagan literary humanism that had been imported from Italy. The great craze was the sonnet sequence: a series of poems tracing the development of a love affair. The form had been

---

11 John Foxe, *Foxe's Book of Martyrs*, Pennsylvania: Whitaker, 1981, p. 184–5.

invented by Dante and Petrarch, who were themselves adapting the courtly love tradition of the troubadours. The loved woman is of course mythologized, as an object of worship. This would be idolatrous, but for the fact that she is, in theory, seen as an agent of God. Following the Neo-platonic tradition, her beauty is an expression of divine beauty. Love is a spiritual discipline, through which the poet gradually learns to overcome carnal desire and love purely. So love poetry is deeply ambiguous: in theory it celebrates the overcoming of sensuality, and the achievement of spiritual enlightenment, but of course there is scope for celebrating the psychological complexities, and sheer thrill, of carnal love along the way.

Spenser's sonnet sequence is sincere, idealistic: he wants to affirm the narrative of physical attraction developing into pure and holy love. He published another poem along with his sonnets in 1595, a triumphant poem about marriage, whose writing coincided with his own wedding. It's worth pausing to consider it, for very few poems are so obviously influential on Milton. Like all of Spenser's poetry, 'Epithalamion' is written in an archaic style, it seems as close to Chaucer as to Milton. He wants to import an atmosphere of medieval purity. This poem is a wedding hymn that follows the progress of the day, from the bridegroom's excited perspective. 'Epithalamion' means 'On the bridal chamber', and the wedding night is the ever-anticipated climax. Despite being archaic, pious and formal, it's strangely sexy. The imagery is largely classical but the feel is more biblical: the stark, simple passion recalls the Song of Songs. After much preamble the bride arrives, and the poet looks on her with wondrous, hungry love. 'Her modest eyes, abashèd to behold / So many gazers, as on her do stare, / Upon the lowly ground affixèd are.' She is described in the primitivist biblical style: 'Her paps lyke lilies budded, / Her snowy neck like to a marble towre . . .' Spenser's genius is to bring out the eroticism intrinsic to virginal purity. This sounds almost paradoxical: we are accustomed to linking eroticism with the opposite of innocence. It also sounds almost taboo: to find innocence sexy. But that half-shocking juxtaposition is the essential aesthetic of the wedding day. A crucial component of *Paradise Lost* is already present in 'Epithalamion': the insight that a religious understanding of sex turns up the eroticism.

This is also a basic concern of Spenser's long unfinished allegorical epic, *The Faerie Queene*. Various knights undertake complex quests, during which they must learn to purify their desire; to see through alluring imitations. The poem's aim, he said, was 'to fashion a gentleman'. It certainly helped to fashion Milton: he imbibed an intensely idealistic view of sex, in which the truly manly hero was proudly chaste. Unlike James Bond, the heroic knight's conquests are not of women but of various temptations. Milton was later to name Spenser as his primary theological, as well as literary influence.

The age of Spenser was not quite dead: one of his friends, Sir Walter Raleigh, was still making the headlines. In 1618, when Milton was nine, he was tried and executed. Raleigh was the all-round heroic courtier, and pioneer of a new sort of cocky patriotism (he is Churchill's spiritual ancestor). He had an instinctive belief in liberty – he saw that this had to be England's imperial idea. He hated Spain's lucrative hold on the Americas, and insisted that England was destined to triumph there instead, being morally superior. Whereas the Spanish colonists were spreading Roman superstition, infecting savages with fresh darkness, England would bring them light. In domestic politics his commitment to liberty was sincere and courageous: he was one of the few courtly voices advocating the highest possible degree of toleration. In 1593, he defended the right of the Brownists to be allowed to worship in peace, and spoke against compulsory attendance at the established Church. As soon as James came to the throne, he saw this cult-figure as a threat and imprisoned him. In 1617, he was allowed to undertake an exploratory voyage in Guiana. On his return he was accused of breaking an international agreement with Spain, and executed. To Milton he was a hero: he loved his *History of the World*, which announced that God's providence was the driving force of global history, that tyrants got their comeuppance, that all the exotic cultures of the world could be subjected to rational scrutiny. It urged the English to spread liberty throughout the world, warning them that they were up against the might of the Turks and the Spanish: 'the one seeking to root out the Christian religion altogether, the other the truth and sincere profession thereof, the one to join all Europe to Asia, the other the rest of all Europe to Spain.'[12] He offered his fellow Englishmen a frail vision: of England serving God's historical will by rising to defeat two evil empires. Milton remained a fan of Raleigh all his life: in middle age he re-published one of his pamphlets.

James considered the book to be 'too sawcie in censuring princes' – and he was right; it elevated the principle of liberty over the monarch's right to rule. Raleigh's execution ended the Elizabethan era; whereas the queen had managed to seem the patroness of Protestant liberty, James seemed threatened by it. He even seemed ready to do Spain's bidding. He had continued to alienate the Puritans, some of whom emigrated. In the year of Milton's birth the group left for Holland who would later cross the Atlantic on the Mayflower. He also alienated Parliament. In 1610, he told them of his divine right once again: 'The state of monarchy is the supremest thing upon earth: for Kings are not only God's lieutenants upon earth, and sit upon God's throne, but even by God himself are called Gods.'[13]

Despite being a canny politician, his behaviour did not live up to this self-image. Court banquets were often drunken riots. At one masque 'everyone from their majesties down got beastly drunk, including the ladies playing Faith, Hope and Charity, who had to be led off stage too "sick and spewing" to say their lines.'[14] He favoured a succession of young Scottish men with whom he may have been sexually involved: he certainly behaved like their jealous older lover. In 1612, his oldest son, Henry, died, which left his less personable son Charles the heir.

James's belief in the divine grandeur of kingship seemed imitative of the Catholic courts of Europe. Was divine-right monarchism a Catholic-leaning ideology? Elizabeth had certainly asserted her divine right, in grand style, but this had been part of a national-Protestant narrative. The aesthetic of royal power was now losing its national feel, seeming to follow the baroque style of the Catholic Continent. The Tudor revolution

---

12   Walter Raleigh, *The History of the World*, ed. G. A. Patrides, London: Macmillan, 1971, p. 395.

13   Quoted in Antonia Fraser, *James I of England and VI of Scotland*, London: Weidenfeld and Nicholson, 1974, p. 98.

14   Charles Carlton, *Charles I, The Personal Monarch*, London: Routledge 1995, p. 6.

had welded royal power to Protestantism. The monarch's divine right was not simply to rule but to forge a Protestant nation. But this narrative was risky: it empowered Puritans, hostile to a top-down established Church. James wanted to keep such people in check, so he emphasized another aspect of the Tudor revolution: the intimate relationship of the crown and the episcopate, summed up in his catchphrase 'no bishop, no king'. The Protestantism of the national church was secondary to its establishment. So he stepped up his attack on Puritanism, especially in Scotland, where the Church was effectively two churches: the Presbyterian 'Kirk', and colonial Anglicanism. He ordered it to celebrate the Christian festivals. In England he issued *The Book of Sports*, which affirmed the right to worldly Sunday entertainments like football, dancing and drinking. The aim was to exclude the Puritans from cultural power.

By 1620, Milton had started at St Paul's school, close by the cathedral. He was proud of the school's humanist origins: it had been founded in 1509 by John Colet, Erasmus' great friend. Its motto, *Fide et Literis* (by faith and learning), was suitably humanist. The High Master, Alexander Gill, was a literary scholar (who particularly admired Spenser), and his son was a poet. The school was dedicated to the boy Jesus, a picture of whom hung over the High Master's chair, and to whom a daily prayer was said:

> Sweet Jesus, my Lord, who, as a boy in the twelfth year of thine age didst dispute in the temple at Jerusalem among the doctors so that they all marveled with amazement at thy superexcellent wisdom, I petition thee that at this thy school, of which thou art protector and defender, wherein I am taught daily in letters and wisdom, that I may chiefly come to know thee Jesus, who art thyself the true wisdom . . . [15]

Thus the precocious youth worshipped the divinely precocious youth. The spiritual ideal of 'the imitation of Christ' is rather dangerous, if you

---

15   Quoted in A. N. Wilson, *The Life of John Milton*, London: Pimlico 1982, p. 10.

think about it: it could lead a young man to flirt with the idea of his exceptional destiny. Milton was fascinated by the pious arrogance of a mere boy who claims superior authority to all priests and teachers – someone even more heroic than Foxe's Luther. He would later imagine Jesus remembering his own boyhood calling.

While he was at St Paul's, the cathedral appointed a new dean: John Donne, who in a previous life had pioneered a new style of clever, risqué, cynical love poetry. He was now a royally favoured preacher, whose sermons combined highly conservative politics with thundering assertions of our fallenness, and our propensity to cosmic treason. Milton was probably impressed by this dramatic, turbulent style of religious rhetoric, which is also to be found in Donne's religious poems. In 1622, James issued his Directions for Preachers, clamping down on dissenting tendencies among the clergy, and announcing new censorship measures, and Donne was chosen to publicize it in a sermon. Milton was surely mindful of what his former tutor, Thomas Young, would think about such measures: did not a power-loving episcopal Church jeopardize the freedom of the Gospel? Though he was conscious of the question, Milton was not the teenage radical type. More likely he admired Donne, and was generally respectful of authority. He was certainly sensitive to the beauty of cathedral worship. He was soon to write that the holy architecture combined with the 'pealing organ blow' and 'the full-voiced choir', has the power to 'Dissolve me into ecstasies, / And bring all heaven before mine eyes.'[16]

Puritan sympathy was also drowned out by the knowledge that his most likely future role was as a priest of the established Church. For surely it was mere folly to fantasize about another, rarer sort of calling. And yet the seed of the idea had been planted – that he was a great poet in the making. Where does ambition of this sort come from? Some of it is nurtured: Milton's father had given him permission to think that his talent was exceptional, that he was destined for something special. And this led him to work on it, to gain a precocious stylistic confidence.

---

16   Milton, 'Il Penseroso' (60–6).

He had one school friend with whom he could share his quiet ambition. Charles Diodati was half-Italian: Milton was attracted by his air of otherness, and also by the family's links to Continental Protestantism. His friend embodied the fusion of Renaissance poetry and Protestant truth that already attracted Milton. They exchanged verses and hatched great literary plans. In his company, and writing to him, Milton felt free to strike literary poses, to express himself. A very close bond developed, perhaps the closest of Milton's life.

In 1625, he started at Christ's College, Cambridge, aged sixteen. It was like transferring to a rigid boarding school, where one was more exposed to the taunts of uncouth types. He was teased for his fastidious, effeminate image, and acquired the nickname 'the lady of Christ's' – enough to drive an undergraduate into a severe breakdown, one might have thought. He was having trouble settling in. Something happened that caused him to fall out with his tutor, and to be briefly suspended.

While back in London he wrote a Latin poem to Charles Diodati: amid lots of classical posturing he expresses dissatisfaction at 'the rushy fens of the Cam', and a love of the urbane bustle of the capital, including its theatre and beautiful girls. Milton might seem an unlikely flâneur, but there is a real vividness to this little sketch of urban thrill. It's generally hard to know how highly to rate these early poems: as well as being in Latin they are encased in grave pastiche, and knowing pretension. Nevertheless one senses clarity and energy, and a stylist's attention to detail.

It is clear that he and Charles had entered into a special sort of friendship – they were soul-mates, and, in a sense, lovers. There was clearly no sex involved, but on the other hand there was a certain amount of sexy literary banter, of camp allusions to Ovid. The relationship was a sort of refuge from heterosexual reality. Does this mean that Milton was homosexually inclined? Not really: it means that he used a playful, platonic homosexuality as a way of deferring adult heterosexuality. Sex clearly alarmed him, yet in order to grow up he had to address it in some way: this was a way. Gay sex was so completely taboo that a special friendship with a man was a safely sexless place to be.[17]

---

17   Anna Beer's recent biography is a good guide to the tradition of platonic male friendship: Anna Beer, *John Milton: Poet, Patriot, Pamphleteer*, London: Bloomsbury 2008, p. 51 and *passim*.

Back in college he managed to find some sort of niche. His skill in Latin earned him the grudging respect of his peers. Intellectual culture was based on rhetorical performance, in Latin: speeches, debates, poetry recitals. Milton forced himself to enter the fray, to acquire an effective public persona. This determination of the private undergraduate to find a public role sets the pattern for his career. He had to force himself to perform a public role. Wain points to a comparison with W. B. Yeats: 'Both were shy, proud men who forced themselves, not without a self-consuming inner delight, to play a part on the public stage. Both were in love with pride – Milton half-consciously, Yeats openly – and both wrote superbly in praise of the proud character.'[18]

During his first year at Cambridge, King James died. He was succeeded by his son Charles I, but also, unofficially, by the Duke of Buckingham, whose macho personality had enthralled James and still enthralled his son. Charles was already unpopular with the Protestant-minded. He had come close to marrying a Spanish princess a few years earlier, and was about to marry a French one, which was nearly as bad. It was rumoured that the marriage treaty involved a softening of the ban on Roman Catholicism. The idea of England as the great Protestant nation had become risible in the last years of James' reign. In 1621, the Palatinate, the German Protestant principality, had been attacked by Spain, sparking the Thirty Years War. James had failed to come to its aid, despite the fact that Prince Frederick was his son-in-law. Foreign policy was purely pragmatic: the idea of furthering international Protestantism was absent. When Charles married Henrietta Maria, a few months into his reign, Protestant fears were confirmed: she had been given the right to raise their children as Roman Catholics until they were thirteen. And her large French entourage included many priests. She was a fervent young Catholic who saw herself as a new Queen Bertha (a medieval French queen who had secured the conversion of the Kentish royal family).

If any setting was going to radicalize a young Protestant it was Cambridge. The university had been the intellectual centre of English Protestantism since Cranmer's day, and the tradition had been revived

---

18   John Wain, 'Strength and Isolation: Pessimistic Notes of a Miltonolater', in Frank Kermode ed., *The Living Milton,* London: Routledge and Kegan Paul, 1960, p. 5.

under Elizabeth, especially by Thomas Cartwright. There was plenty of Puritan zeal around, looking for recruits – and Christ's was perhaps the most radical college of all.[19] But Milton was in no hurry to be radicalized. Poetry came first.

At the beginning of his second year at Cambridge, he wrote an elegy to Lancelot Andrewes, the Bishop of Winchester, and leader of the high Church party. It is the verbal equivalent of a baroque sculpture, an excuse to showcase his decorative poetic skill. The next month there was another such opportunity when the Bishop of Ely died. He did not have to write either elegy, and a convinced Puritan would not have. He was, however a convinced Protestant, and he showed it in a long poem on the Gunpowder Plot, written for a college celebration. It is a mini-epic, again in Latin, starring Satan, who is furious at Britain's Protestantism: 'this nation alone is rebellious against me, scornful of my yoke and stronger than my art.' He flies off to Rome, where he persuades the Pope to launch a terrorist plot. (In reality, of course the pope was about as responsible for 5 November as Saddam Hussein was for 11 September.) Satan goes back to hell, which is sketched by Milton with obvious relish: 'Here for ever sits black Guile with twisted eyes, ... and pale Horror flutters about the place ...' There is an almost Gothic pleasure in this depiction. He enjoys imagining the extremity of mythological evil. He also enjoys dramatizing it, narrating it through speeches; giving voice to Satan. The poem combines two of his major influences: it echoes Foxe's national-Protestant triumphalism, and Spenser's vivid narrative poetry.

A few months later he wrote a poetic letter to his former tutor Thomas Young, now ministering to Puritan exiles in Hamburg. It imagines a goddess carrying the missive over to Germany, whose landscape is imagined in classical terms, and finding its recipient: 'There lives, in the lustre of his primitive piety, a pastor well fitted to feed his Christian flock.' Milton recalls their relationship: 'Under his tutelage I first visited the retreats of Aonia and the hallowed glades of the twin-peaked mountain, and drained Pierian waters, and by Clio's favour I thrice wet my happy lips with

---

19 Quentin Skinner, 'The Generation of John Milton', in *Christ's: A Cambridge College over Five Centuries*, ed. by David Reynolds, London: Macmillan, 2005, p. 45.

Castalian wine.' The 'twin-peaked mountain' is Parnassus. It ought to be jarring, the idea that this austere pastor also initiates boys in pagan exoticism, but it is not. The paganism is a harmonious, harmless backdrop. And it is surprisingly beautiful, like a Claude Lorraine painting. In a few confident details, he conjures up the virtual world of classical myth. After this excited recollection of his own education, Milton returns to imagining Young in his pastoral work, reading the Bible with his parishioners. What is remarkable is Milton's confidence in incorporating classical aestheticism in a poem about Christian purity. He acknowledges the beauty of this tradition, and re-performs it, yet he is not in thrall to it. For he has superior regard for the logic and rhetoric of Protestantism. This poem ends by telling Young not to fear the spread of the Thirty Years War through Germany, 'For you shall be secure under the bright shield of God ...' He reminds him of an Old Testament story in which God scatters the enemy army by creating an aural illusion of the Israelite cavalry coming. Why does Milton choose this, out of hundreds of stories of divine power? Because, in his hands, it is about the power of poetry. Milton re-creates the illusory noise in a few lines of vivid poetry. He is telling his former teacher: this is how I understand my gift; it participates in the mighty Word of God. It is because he has such confidence in this agenda that he is so calm about pagan aestheticism: he can engage in it with a smile, knowing that it will serve, not jeopardize, his graver purpose.

His budding genius, then, cannot be separated from an extreme rhetorical confidence, which is faith-based. Powerful speech is always mythically powerful, caught up in the grand narrative of the self-communication of God. This theme is central to the first major English poem of his career, 'On the Morning of Christ's Nativity', written at Christmas 1629. It is like an early Renaissance painting, in which the stark simplicity of the nativity is asserted. Christmas involves a pastoral aesthetic: the setting is rural and rude. God spurns the deluxe palaces in which He could be born, in favour of a shed. The cast includes peasants. Yet there is unparalleled beauty here: that is the message of Christmas, and of the pastoral mode. Milton does not immediately begin in this mode: his prologue is grand and grave. And then the main part of the poem, 'the hymn' begins, with added purity. In its earthy, innocent ritual feel, it refers back to Spenser's 'Epithalamion'. There is an analogous event that's being hymned: an event to do with shocking human nakedness. It is worth underlining that his first major poem has a ritual, liturgical shape. It is not just a poem about the nativity, written from a huge distance: it is a poem that claims to participate in the event it represents.

Christ's birth is presented as a cosmic exorcism: it means the downfall of the demonic deities that have hitherto ruled. The poem climaxes in a long description of pagan gods being flushed out from their shrines; sent packing. There is lot of Gothic howling as sprites are expelled from scenic glades, and 'With flow'r-inwoven tresses torn / The nymphs in twilight shade of tangled thickets mourn.' Moloch has left his fiery shrine, to the dismay of his priests: 'In vain with cymbals' ring / They call the grisly king, / In dismal dance about the furnace blue.' Osiris has similarly taken flight: 'He feels from Judah's land / The dreaded Infant's hand … Our Babe, to show his Godhead true, / Can in his swaddling bands control the whole damned crew.' In the prophetic bluntness of the short-lined couplets Milton hammers home the cosmic victory of Christ. It is a celebration of divine power, divine violence. Yet in the final stanza we are suddenly reminded of the form this cosmic victory takes: 'But see, the Virgin blest / Hath laid her babe to rest …'. Of course Milton relishes depicting the pagan religiosity that's overcome, but that doesn't mean his allegiance lies there, that he is really of the pagans' party without knowing it. There is no contradiction between his love of the exotic classical world and his conviction that it is overcome, defeated by Christ. The poem is like a Roman triumph in which the exotic natives from far colonies are paraded through the street. Their exotic otherness is celebrated – because subordinated. This poem is the first real proof, in English, of his exceptional ability to make rather ordinary words into strangely elegant poetry. 'Of all the English poets he is the one for whom sudden beauty in diction seems most inevitable, in whom you never know under what incongruous conditions beauty at white-heat will not appear, shining through an immortal line.'[20]

---

20   Hilaire Belloc, *Milton*, London: Cassell 1935, p. 8.

In this poem the poet claims to be the mouthpiece of the 'Heav'nly Muse', more of a pagan than a Christian entity. Milton's confident straddling of pagan and Christian demands further reflection. How did the undergraduate see the relationship between Christianity and literature? We must take a few steps back, and consider the entire tradition from which he came.

Classical literature was never fully eclipsed by Christian orthodoxy. Some early Fathers such as Justin Martyr tried to read all of classical philosophy and literature as a gift from God, to be gradually decoded by the Christian key. Others attributed these things to the Devil. A compromise emerged: the Church did not entirely condemn pagan literature yet treated it with caution. In the fourth century, St Jerome felt guilty about his love of Cicero (he dreamed that God rebuked him for it, calling him more of a Ciceronian than a Christian), and in the next century Augustine treated classical literature with a high-minded disdain that veiled an uneasy attraction. The influence of the classics receded with the fall of Rome in the fifth century, yet it never entirely ceased to flow. Throughout the Dark Ages there were endless nods to classical antiquity in the courts of such kings as Alfred and Charlemagne. The Christian king was a descendant of Constantine, who combined classical and Christian traditions. Medieval literary culture always had this neo-classical component. And of course it was fused with biblical and devotional forms, and also with local pagan traditions of story and song. These pagan influences were ordered, baptized, subjected to the master-narrative of Christendom. *Beowulf* is the baptism of a pagan monster myth, for example. Literary culture was defined by syncretism, the combining of one religious tradition with another. And of course the Christian myth was always officially dominant.

This continues in the literary humanism of early fourteenth century Florence. Dante's vernacular allegory-epic appropriates classical mythology, brings it into the Christian story. But of course this appropriation is dangerous: the old myths are re-animated. Virgil is revered, despite his exclusion from salvation. Renaissance poetry is fraught with this ambiguity. In Christianizing pagan myths, it also revives their pagan appeal. Literary humanism claims to be unaware of this danger: the poet is the loyal servant of Christendom, and therefore only ironic in his imitation of idolatrous love poetry and so on. Literary humanism is defined by this confidence that Christian culture can accommodate a pagan revival in its midst. But sometimes the show of confidence wavers: Chaucer was uneasy about the worldliness of poetry. Poets such as Boccaccio and Rabelais seemed to leave piety behind, and to open the door to Ovidian sensuality.

Under the Tudors, Renaissance poetry became a fixture of court life. Wyatt imported the Italian sonnet to Henry's court, and with it the intellectual craze of Florentine Platonism. Following Ficino and Pico della Mirandella, Tudor intellectuals were excited by the Neoplatonic notion of divine ascent: the practice of rational virtue ennobles us, makes us almost godlike. Poetry was seen as a divine activity, a participation in God. This is the first serious neoclassical tradition in English intellectual life. Again it is a form of syncretism: the Christian myth is combined with a classical one. And the medieval courtly love tradition is also incorporated. Devotion to the loved one blurs with devotion to the divine ideal.

In Elizabeth's reign Sir Philip Sidney wrote a prose treatise, *An Apology for Poetry*, that follows Florentine thinking. It explains that poetry is the most creative of art forms: instead of merely copying nature, the poet can 'grow in effect into another nature, in making things either better than Nature bringeth forth, or, quite anew, forms such as never were.'[21] He can create a virtual world, a better world. This power is not to be feared from a Christian perspective; instead it is a proof that we are made in the image of the creator God; it is also proof of the doctrine of the fall, for 'our erected wit maketh us know what perfection is, and yet our infected will keepeth us from reaching into it.'[22] As we shall see, this insight is particularly relevant to *Paradise Lost*, which plays with perfection's distance. And this virtual world can inspire us to virtue, by making goodness seem attractive. The poet outdoes the philosopher: he not only shows the way to live, but 'giveth so sweet a prospect into the way, as will

21   Sir Philip Sidney, *An Apology for Poetry*, ed. by Geoffrey Shepherd, Manchester: Manchester University Press, 1975, p. 100.
22   Ibid., p. 101.

entice any man to enter into it.'[23] For example epic heroes 'maketh magnanimity and justice shine throughout all misty fearfulness and foggy desires.'[24]

But Sidney evades the problem of pagan aestheticism. Surely the virtual world of a pagan poem is dangerous to Christian orthodoxy? There's a strong hint of this in Marlowe's play *Doctor Faustus*. The demonically-assisted magician resurrects Helen of Troy, and idolizes her. The suggestion is that the classical world, recreated through art, is fraught with danger. It is an alternative, illicit form of desire, a threat to moral and religious order. And this awareness seeps into early seventeenth century poetry. Donne breaks with the air of flippancy that surrounds Elizabethan poetry, importing a new psychological realism (influenced by Marlowe and Shakespeare). His initial persona is a rather rakish version of the Platonic lover. He uses the high idealism of poetic convention as a foil for witty, caddish worldliness, into which sharp melancholy intrudes. He then repents of this voice, and decides that poetry is for communicating the true pathos of faith. Once poetry is directly related to religion the potential for conflict has to be faced. God's Word can tolerate no alternative authority, and the cult of pagan literature is such an alternative. Donne's younger contemporary George Herbert directly challenges the pagan leaning of poetry. Why should poetry be neo-pagan, he asks in an early sonnet: 'Doth Poetry / Wear Venus' livery? Only serve her turn? / Why are not sonnets made of Thee, and lays / Upon Thine altar burnt? Cannot Thy love / Heighten a spirit to sound out Thy praise / As well as any she?' It is not an original insight that humanist poetics is idolatrous; what is new is objecting to this, taking the idolatry seriously. The two 'Jordan' poems in *The Temple* (published 1633) return to the question: 'Is there in truth no beautie?' asks the first, and the next underlines the point; faith entails an aesthetic devoid of artifice. Pagan poetry is likened to the harlot of Proverbs. Like Donne, Herbert is concerned to demonstrate that faith is the truly serious psychological drama, the site of beauty as well as truth.

---

23   Ibid., p. 113.
24   Ibid., p. 119.

So in the early seventeenth century there is some reaction against the neo-paganism of humanist poetics, partly due to the growing impact of Puritanism. But the boat is not really rocked. The Elizabethan instinct for syncretism continues in the most influential poetic school, led by Ben Jonson. Indeed he takes classical models more seriously than any English predecessor, effectively launching the Augustan era in English literature. He worked at court, writing masques; he was a new sort of secular-professional poet. To Jonson and his followers, religious themes ought not to dominate poetry: devotional poetry was just one genre, and it should know its place. Herrick is a good example of this attitude: though a priest, his poetry was more interested in imitating Horace and Juvenal than promoting Christian faith.

The Nativity Ode suggests that Milton wants to baptize poetry, yet not with the bluntness of later Donne or Herbert, that frowns on sensuous aestheticism. He wants to demonstrate that poetic beauty is no threat to the absolute majesty of the Word. The poem also shows Milton's interest in eschatology, in the idea of God's final cosmic victory that wraps up history, and brings heaven on earth – a state in which, as Isaiah puts it, there will be no more tears, and as Paul puts it, God will be all in all. He wants to communicate this biblical hope, make it new. He soon writes another poem, 'On Time' (1632), that confirms this interest: it is a beautiful imagining of the promised end.

> . . . For when as each thing bad thou [Time] hast entombed,
> And last of all thy greedy self consumed,
> Then long eternity shall greet our bliss
> With an individual kiss;
> And joy shall overtake us as a flood,
> When every thing that is sincerely good
> And perfectly divine,
> With Truth, and Peace, and Love, shall ever shine . . .

The trick of this is a sort of grand innocence, a majestically bold simplicity. The subject matter overlaps with Donne's sonnet 'Death be not proud', but Donne's sonnet is too full of messy human psychology. Milton sees

that the cosmic victory must be imagined as easy, elegant, utterly beauti-
ful. As we shall see, Milton's eschatological emphasis persists throughout
his career. He rightly sees that this is the very essence of Christian faith.
Does that mean that he really believes in the lurid predictions of the Book
of Revelation? Well, it is impossible to believe in all that literally; it is all
too obviously poetic. The point is that he affirms the thrust of such bibli-
cal rhetoric, by re-performing it.

He finally left Cambridge in the summer of 1632, unordained. He
might have been expecting to be offered a fellowship, but he was not
(probably a sign that he was detached from college politics, a bad
networker). Why had he held back from ordination? Was it that he had
extreme Puritan views, and could not accept the compromise of Anglican
ordination? There is no evidence of such views yet: he was probably
ambivalent about Puritanism, which he knew to be capable of crude
rigidity. It also seems that he was a bit detached from the fray. Like
many young intellectuals he probably found political (which includes
ecclesiastical) rhetoric depressingly trite: how can intelligent adults bring
themselves to invest mundane issues with such passion? There are no
grounds for thinking that the anti-episcopal cause excited him. He pre-
sumably saw bishops as part of the order of things, part of the English
'middle way'. The established Church, with its bishops, had worked well
enough under Elizabeth, making England the great Protestant nation –
why should it now be dismissed as structurally unsound? On the other
hand, he knew that the Church was changing. It was undergoing a high
church revolution, known as Arminianism.

To explain this rather unhelpful term we must backtrack a bit, and
briefly refer to the religious situation in Holland. In the 1570s, the
Northern Netherlands, the United Provinces, won its independence from
Spain, through a bloody war of resistance. Calvinism had been a huge
factor in the struggle, and a Calvinist church established itself in the new
state. But it met strong liberal opposition: the liberal party (dubbed
Libertines by their Calvinist opponents) argued for a high level of tolera-
tion (including of a well-established Jewish community). In the 1590s,
the Dutch church began to split: there arose a form of Calvinism, or post-
Calvinism, more suited to a tolerant state; it came from a theologian

called Arminius, who questioned the fine print of predestination. He and his followers wanted a church with a looser conception of orthodoxy, a willingness to rethink. His cause was taken up by those who wanted to see the power of the church curtailed, who feared Calvinism's totalitarian tendency. This liberal party began to have international influence: in the early part of James' reign, this movement was influential in the English Church, largely, thanks to the humanist thinker Hugo Grotius. James was sympathetic, for Arminianism seemed a counterweight to Puritan extremism. Yet many churchmen, including the Archbishop of Canterbury, George Abbot, were wary, warning that such liberalism led to Socinianism, the denial of the Trinity.

In 1618, the conservatives in the Dutch church won the upper hand, and staged a theological conference to expel the liberals. The Synod of Dordt, a large international Protestant event, insisted that the doctrine of predestination was sacrosanct, that Arminius was therefore a heretic. Calvinism became a tighter system than ever. The Church of England officially signed up to Dordt's decision, which exposed its ideological confusion. Its hierarchy was battling dogmatic Calvinism, and yet it officially sided with the dogmatic Calvinism of the Dutch.

The Synod of Dordt seemed proof that liberal Calvinism was chimerical. Even in liberal Holland, the Reformed tradition ended up imitating the rigidity of Geneva. Liberal Protestantism seemed a frail thing, vulnerable to new assertions of 'orthodoxy'. Protestantism seemed to need to take fundamentalist form – partly to keep the Counter-Reformation at bay, and partly to harden itself against semi-agnostic rationalism.

A sector of the Church of England continued to rally under the 'Arminian' banner. What united this grouping was its hatred of the hardline Calvinism that had triumphed in Holland. It brought together Erasmian-type liberals and high church Anglicans, full of a semi-Catholic sensibility that emphasized order, hierarchy, and tradition (it makes sense to call them Anglo-Catholics, though the term is anachronistic). In effect, the fear of Calvinism led to a marriage of convenience between liberals and Anglo-Catholics. (Incidentally, something very similar happened in the Church of England in the 1990s: the rise of Evangelicalism led to the formation of a liberal Catholic counterforce.) This party was actually dominated by the Anglo-Catholics – people such as Lancelot Andrewes who insisted that episcopacy was divinely ordained. In the English context, then, 'Arminian' became a misleading term, for its influential advocates were not so much liberal Calvinists, like Arminius himself had been, but Catholic Anglicans, of the sort later known as Anglo-Catholics.

Naturally enough, the Arminians were royally favoured. James saw their 'high' account of the Church as the proper accompaniment of a powerful monarchy. He wanted a proudly episcopal Church, rather than a Calvinist one. But he was canny enough to play carefully. His son was not: when Charles succeeded in 1625, the royal favouring of the Arminians became blatant. There was immediately a controversy surrounding a royal chaplain, Richard Montague: he had written against Calvinism with such vigour that Parliament objected, and demanded his removal. Charles gave him uncompromising support: a sign of things to come. Charles succeeded with a very fixed idea about the grandeur of monarchy: it should be expressed in lavish and meticulous religious rituals. He saw the royal chapel as a beacon, to guide the Church as a whole. The coming trouble was very largely of his own making: 'although Charles I was not attempting to reintroduce popery he was certainly attempting to mould the Anglican Church into a Catholic identity to rival the national Churches of Spain and France.'[25]

It was little surprise that he promoted William Laud, who had emerged as the leader of the high Church party. Laud was, alongside Cranmer, the most influential Anglican leader ever. His insistence that this Church should be more Catholic than Protestant in look and feel was defeated in the short term, but triumphed in the long term. He was a short, fat man of homosexual inclination, widely despised for his low birth and his officious managerial style. He got things done. He set about putting this ramshackle Church in order.

His theological vision was rooted in his deep and passionate study of the early church fathers. What he learned from them was that the unity of

---

25 Julian Davies, *The Caroline Captivity of the Church: Charles I and the Remoulding of Anglicanism 1625–41*, Oxford: Clarendon 1992, p. 315.

the Church is rooted in the authority of the bishop. Unless the hierarchy is revered, and the bishop is allowed to enforce uniformity of practice, the Church will fragment. 'Unity cannot long continue in the Church where uniformity is shut out at the church door',[26] he said. His reforms were primarily a matter of enforcing existing church law, and ensuring that all services really followed the Book of Common Prayer, rather than using it as a rough guide. He was genuinely idealistic: he wanted to create a nation-wide culture of liturgical serenity and order, to spread this saving form of theatre into every corner of the kingdom. Every parishioner deserved beautiful sacramental worship. The aesthetic dimension is important: Laud's creed is often summed up in the phrase 'the beauty of holiness.' He saw liturgical beauty as the key channel of religious truth. But in this context 'beauty' is tied to authoritarianism. For this beauty consists in an order that must be imposed. Laud's reformation meant checking up on every parish, disciplining those priests with obstructive ideas of their own, showing dissenters zero tolerance.

Laud's form of Christian enthusiasm was not some odd aberration. It was Catholicism, non-Roman Catholicism. Catholicism means belief in the authority of the institutional church. This 'high' model was the destiny of the English Church, he insisted. And he was basically right. In subsequent centuries, the English Church gravitated back to this model, despite massive Protestant resistance. It is worth observing that there is a lot in common between Laud and the present Archbishop of Canterbury, Rowan Williams. Like Laud, he is excited by a quasi-aesthetic ideal of early church purity – and he too sees the bishop's authority as pivotal to the Catholic tradition. He agrees with Laud that a Church is united by its shared sacramental life, and by the authority of its hierarchy. (His attachment to this Catholic model has of course proved far stronger than his liberalism.)

Of course Puritans accused him of being a Roman Catholic in all but name, but in a sense this missed the point. He thought that the English Church had a special mission, to be a *superior* model of ecclesiastical order to Rome, which remained tainted by abuses. But of course the

---

26 Archishop Laud, quoted in ibid. [i.e Davies 1992], p. 61.

model was essentially Roman Catholic, in its emphasis on the authority of the institution.

When Charles appointed him to Canterbury in 1633, Laud stepped up his reforming work, like 'an old man in a hurry'.[27] He launched an intra-Anglican Counter-Reformation. He strongly opposed the prominence of preaching and the neglect of ritual propriety. The structure of actual churches was changed: the altar was given new prominence; it became mandatory to place a rail in front of it, before which communicants should kneel. The point was to impress people with the power of the institution, and its priesthood. Ecclesiastical order was God's primary medium of revelation; every service should be an awesome performance of this power. The Church must employ the finest music and art to secure the effect. The Counter-Reformation weapon of choral polyphony was imported.

Laud tightened the Church's monopoly on Christian culture. Puritanism had developed practices that were semi-detached from the official Church. Most obviously, there was a thriving culture of preaching that was only weakly regulated. There were preachers known as 'lecturers' who were not ordained yet often had large followings. Their relationship with the official Church was contentious: the Puritan clergy backed them, and indeed funded them, but the traditionalists resented their popularity. (There is an analogy with the Alpha movement that became a major force within Anglicanism in the 1990s.) In some cases the lecturers seem to have been cult figures, not unrelated to the televangelists of the US. One bishop likened them to 'ballad singers and happy-horse sellers' for their ability to draw a gullible crowd.[28] Under James, this para-ecclesial culture had been allowed to grow: now it was drastically pruned, by a strict enforcement of the Royal Instructions of 1629.

Laud's approach was to restore full authority to the bishops. But of course in doing so, he brought England's ancient anti-clerical tradition to the surface. What he meant to say was that bishops should be the lynchpins of the Church, as in the first Christian centuries: they should

---

27 Mark Kishlansky, *A Monarchy Transformed: Britain 1603–1714,* London: Penguin 1996, p. 129.
28 Davies 1992, p. 130.

be sacramental figures, living symbols of holy order. But what most people heard him saying is that bishops should be more powerful, more respected, richer. Laud failed to see the extent of this negative perception. In his mind, it was obvious that the grandeur of the bishop was for the sake of the glorification of the Church; he assumed that the vast majority would concur, would take pride in a newly majestic Church. But of course bishops were powerful civil servants, and major landowners. They had large retinues. For example the bishop of Norwich, a middle ranking bishop, had a household of at least forty, 'including a dwarf and a trumpeter'.[29]

So the ascent of Laud confirmed Milton's decision against ordination. He could not find his vocation in a Church that was in the grip of an anti-Protestant reaction. As he later said, he had been 'church-outed by the prelates': forced out of his expected career by the rise of the Catholic reactionaries. But this is a bit too neat. In reality it is hard to imagine him placing himself under orders in any Church, even a more proudly Protestant one. He was temperamentally suited to being an outsider.

So what would he do instead? He moved to his parents' house in Hammersmith, and soon moved with them to a country house near Windsor, and kept on reading, thinking, writing. To what end? At around this time, he wrote a Latin poem to his father, in which he declared his determination to be a poet. 'Divine song . . . proclaims the celestial source of the human mind', he insists, and then he repeatedly asserts the quasi-physical *power* of poetry. It 'has the power to stir the trembling depths of Tartarus and to bind the gods below, and it chains the unfeeling shades with triple adamant.' It was through his song that Orpheus 'held back rivers, gave ears to the oak trees, and drew tears from the shades of the dead. Such fame he owes to his song.' He is persuading his father that his poetic ambition is not a retreat from manly life, but a way of achieving heroic influence. And he reminds his father that he is complicit in his son's self-understanding: instead of pressuring him to think about a career, he had funded his education. You chose to fund my literary studies, he is

---

29   Collinson 1982, p. 71.

saying, so don't be surprised that my adult passion is for literature, not for being a businessman, or for the 'noisy stupidity' of the law. He concludes, with great arrogance and great truth, that his father will be remembered for nurturing a poetic genius.

Can anyone in their early twenties really be so confident? Surely there was a shadow side to this confidence, a terrible fear that he was cornering himself into an absurdly pretentious role, that he was developing a dangerous arrogance, with no guarantee that it would serve any good purpose. Perhaps this underlies his famous affinity with Satan, this nagging doubt that his 'vocation' was an illusion of demonic proportions.

We know that he felt frustrated, that he struggled to have faith in his calling. In one sonnet, he worries that his youth is fast passing, and he's made no tangible progress. He is, to borrow from Hopkins, 'Time's eunuch', watching the productivity of his peers from the wings. But he should not be anxious, he tells himself, for his destiny, 'however mean or high', is in God's hands: 'All is, if I have grace to use it so, / As ever in my great Task-Master's eye.' This unusual choice of divine name, which refers to the parable of the talents, seems to respond to the perception that he is work-shy: actually I work for God, he says, which is not such an easy option as it might look. This poem shows some of Milton's major themes taking root in his soul: patience, obedience, trust.

A letter survives in which he responds to a friend's advice to get a job; to do something more than eternal studying (it was probably Young, advising him to hurry up and get ordained). But I'm not just studying for the sake of it, he replies: 'if it were no more but the mere love of learning, whether it proceed from a principle bad, good, or natural, it could not have held out thus long against so strong opposition on the other side of every kind.' He is insisting, in a slightly guarded way, that his life is not about pleasure-seeking; it's hard work, rooted in hard psychological struggle.

Milton was one of the first people to scorn all known career paths on the grounds that he was meant to be a 'writer'. There were almost no professional writers, and the world somehow even survived without professional journalists. A few people scraped a living from writing for the theatre, as Shakespeare had, but this wasn't Milton's style. And yet it was a form of theatre that offered the next stepping-stone in his strange career. The musician Henry Lawes had somehow got wind of Milton's poetic talent: in 1634, he asked him to write the words for a new masque. Masques were all the rage at court: the enthusiasm of Charles and Henrietta Maria had turned this feature of court life into a sort of cult, whose temple was Inigo Jones's new Banqueting Hall at Whitehall. The purpose of theses masques was simply to glorify the monarch, as a chivalric paragon. Away from court, masques might be less crudely prop-agandist, though they were still likely to celebrate something, to be dramatic expressions of an idea. They dispensed with the sustained real-ism of theatre, in order to incorporate song, dance, pageantry.

The new masque was to celebrate the aristocrat Thomas Egerton's inauguration as the Lord President of Wales and leader of the Council of the Marches; it was to be staged at his new seat, Ludlow Castle. It's not quite clear how Milton got away with writing something that bears no obvious relation to the event. The masque he wrote is a celebration of chastity; a warning against the demonic sexual temptation embodied by its villain, Comus. It basically consists of some pretty scene-setting, remi-niscent of one of Shakespeare's enchanted forests, followed by a rhetorical contest between the chaste heroine, the Lady, and the demonic Comus, a sketch for Satan.

It's a dangerous game, representing the attraction of evil – especially sexual evil. When Comus first appears, a stage-direction tells us that he is accompanied by 'a rout of monsters headed like sundry sorts of wild beasts, but otherwise like men and women, their apparel glistening. They come in making a riotous and unruly noise, with torches in their hands.' Milton obviously intends the audience to be thrilled by the sudden pagan primitivity. Comus starts praising revelry, and unfettered desire: he is the ancestor of the rock-god – he soon flaunts a disturbing Jagger-Bowie-type androgyny.

He tricks the Lady into following him to his luxurious palace. He urges her to give herself to him; she resists. Her rhetoric might be plain, lacking the sexy charm of her adversary, but she knows she is right, and trusts that she will triumph. It's a counter-erotic rhetoric. She rebukes him, with lofty head-girl confidence, utterly refusing to be impressed by his

while, and now seizes his chance. Maybe the death of his friend has brought a new sense of urgency, a new sense that he has to get off the fence and express his growing antipathy to the Church.

Through including this passage in his elegy, Milton places himself in the tradition of literary anticlericalism. In the fourteenth century, this tradition was particularly strong: it was fed by Wycliffe's proto-Protestant movement, which became known as Lollardy, and by the tradition of mystical writing. The anticlerical poet echoes the figure of the prophet. In the Old Testament the prophet questions the adequacy of the worship that he witnesses. Sometimes he directly denounces the cult that claims to serve God. And he dares to claim that the voice of God speaks through him. Judeo-Christian tradition is always haunted by the possibility that an authorial voice claiming to be divinely inspired will seek to pull down the complex structures of religion. And vernacular literature threatens to breed such voices. It is a threat to religious institutionalism, cultic practice, orthodoxy.

This anticlerical outburst, in the midst of an elegy, is a marker of Milton's poetic trajectory. While an undergraduate he would have been happy to write a straightforward pastoral elegy, an exercise in neo-paganism. But now his most serious literary urge is to experiment with prophetic rhetoric. Here is an opportunity to update the tradition of English anti-clericalism. Maybe the crisis in the English church offers a prophetic rhetorician a rich seam of material. Is this sort of utterance what his gift is for?

3

Taking Sides

On 1 January 1950, Che Guevara left his native Argentina, and took a long motorbike trip round South America. On his travels he found his vocation. Being away from home sharpened his engagement with political ideas. It was the same for Milton (minus the motorbike). It was while traveling on the Continent for a year and a half that he began to understand the full extent of his vocation. He was not simply a poet, who tended towards religious themes. His poetry had to be fully and explicitly committed to the true, progressive cause. The true, progressive cause was Protestantism. He came to understand that Protestantism was intrinsically liberty-loving. On one level, he had always known this: he had learned it as a boy from Foxe and Raleigh and other Elizabethan writers. On one level, his entire culture took it for granted. But that was the problem: it was taken for granted, instead of being properly asserted, propagated and celebrated. When Milton returned to England, he had a clear sense of mission: to renew the Reformation, through showing, with unprecedented clarity, that the causes of Protestantism and liberty were ultimately *the same thing*. Before now, his vocation was literary (with a religious twist). It now extended to ideas.

He embarked on an early version of the Grand Tour, but the emphasis was not on art and architecture but literature and ideas (and his great aesthetic passion beside poetry: music). His first stop, in the spring of 1638, was Paris. Here he met the Dutch thinker Hugo Grotius, who, as we have briefly seen, was the leading theorist of liberal Protestantism. His liberal views had forced him into exile from Holland, where fundamentalist Calvinism reigned. Milton was already a fan: Grotius was the man he most wanted to meet in Paris. And it is likely that the meeting was pivotal in Milton's development; that he came away feeling that his calling was more theological, and political, than poetic. For thirty years Grotius had been pushing the same big idea: a liberal Protestant movement, based on the thought of Arminius, could re-unite Europe. Grotius's other hero was Erasmus, and he himself was a sort of post-Reformation Erasmus, who had faith in a moderate, inclusive Protestantism rather than Catholicism. Unfortunately the most influential Protestants, the Calvinists, saw him as something between a crypto-papist and a crypto-atheist. He doubtless reiterated to Milton his vision, that Arminianism 'could provide a basis upon which liberal Calvinists in the Netherlands, Anglicans in England, Gallicans and liberal Huguenots in France, could unite leaving the extremists of popery and Puritanism to wither gradually away. He also believed that the leadership in such a movement naturally belonged to England.'[34] Over the coming year, this vision seeped deeper into Milton's mind – he began to feel that there was an ideological cause so grand and urgent that poetry was no longer the priority.

He went on to Italy, visiting Genoa and then moving on to Florence. He had dreamed of this place since boyhood; he himself was a child of the Renaissance that had begun here. Northern Italy was to him the very home of civilization. And yet things were less straightforward. Because the Reformation had not happened here, and was instead violently suppressed, this entire culture was a case of arrested development. It had led the world in art, literature and science, and then, when the crucial religious revolution arrived, it had turned against it. So Milton's feelings about all the artistic splendour that he encountered were mixed: was it all evidence of the triumph of aesthetics, and arid intellectualism, over truth?

---

34   Hugh Trevor-Roper, *Catholics, Anglicans and Puritans: Seventeenth-Century Essays*, London: Fontana, 1987, p. 53.

To his delight, he was welcomed by a literary circle in Florence, and treated as a bit of a celebrity. The city had an earnest intellectual culture that Cambridge had lacked; he felt able to relax in a new way, to drop his prickly defences and be relatively charming to those he met. Here he was not dismissed as an effeminate oddball. His Latin and Italian poems were taken seriously: he had never been granted such recognition in England. This was a turning-point: for years he had been trying to believe in his identity as a poet, and here it was fully credited. A few years later he wrote a sketch of his poetic career so far, and put great emphasis on his good reception in Italy: the poems he showed his new friends 'met with acceptance above what was looked for', and some were 'received with written encomiums, which the Italian is not forward to bestow on men of this side the Alps.'[35] This recognition made him more attentive to 'an inward prompting which now grew daily upon me, that by labour and intense study (which I take to be my portions in this life), joined with the strong propensity of nature, I might perhaps leave something so written to aftertimes, as they should not willingly let it die.'[36] Of course it was not a new thought, that he would be a great writer, but he now entered a new phase of believing it to be possible, and upping the stakes.

His ambiguous delight in Italian magnificence was even more pronounced in Rome. The city was the source of western civilization: there was evidence in every street and square and column and grand fountain – but the source was poisoned. The city was a massive assertion of worldly and religious power, but this power had lost its mooring in Christian truth. Luther had come here a hundred and thirty years earlier, and sensed this dislocation: the grand theatre of worship and pilgrimage was obscuring the message of Jesus. Milton had been reared on a century of Protestant polemics against this city, and yet he was more affected than he expected to be by the sheer visceral kick of the place, the atmosphere of grand religious purpose, like a human reflection of celestial order. Protestant propaganda does not prepare one for this.

---

35   Milton, *The Reason of Church Government*, CPW vol. 1, p. 812.
36   Ibid., p. 352.

He became more aware of Rome's appeal, and of the need to harden himself against it. What really impressed and chilled him was Rome's confidence. Instead of being shaken by the defiance of northern Europe, the papacy calmly expected to regain its supremacy there soon. This gave Milton a fresh sense of defiance. He felt himself to be the representative of Protestantism, who had to assert it even in the jaws of the beast. What had to be asserted, clearly and calmly, was that the grandeur of Rome was tainted by its authoritarianism. Its ubiquitous priests doubled as a secret police force, stifling intellectual freedom. The proof of its inferiority to Protestantism was its reliance on the Inquisition. Most of the intellectuals he met were nervous of the Church, and envied the freedom of the English. And it struck him that he had taken such freedom too much for granted. It had to be passionately defended, lest England slip back into unfreedom. He refused to hide his staunchly Protestant views – not for him the careful academic equivocation of his hosts. As a consequence the authorities began to resent his presence: friends advised him to keep his head down if he wanted to get home safely. His indignation at Roman intransigence was heightened by a meeting in Florence with the elderly Galileo. Here was the essential victim of the Inquisition, forced to hide his light away, lest it embarrass church orthodoxy.

On the way home he stopped in Geneva, to stay with Charles Diodati's uncle. Meeting Giovanni Diodati confirmed his new enthusiasm for the international Protestant cause. Like Grotius, Diodati was part of a Continental Protestant-humanist network. He dreamed of his native Italy turning Protestant. Both men excited Milton with their sense of world-historical purpose, with their sense that Protestantism was a cause that had to be fought for, intellectually as well as politically. It is likely that the keenest Protestants he had encountered back in England were less intellectually impressive, to put it mildly – their zeal tended to be simplistic, strident. On the Continent he gained a new sense that Protestantism could lay claim to the intellectual high-ground.

And he started wondering why England had allowed its leadership of the Protestant cause to lapse. It was the only premier-league state in Europe to have turned Protestant, so why had it become a spectator in the international struggle? Where was the heroic idealism of the Elizabethan age? It had migrated to the Continent, to Gustavus Adolphus and other Protestant princes. Was it not time to restore national Protestant pride? But instead, the Church of England was lost in admiration for Rome.

At some point on his return journey he learned that his best friend, Charles Diodati, had died – perhaps he was told the news by Charles' uncle. The grief confirmed his sense of sudden entry into manhood, of putting away childish things. He soon started an elegy to Charles, cast as the shepherd Damon, that served to draw a line under what could be called the Greek phase of his development. The poem even states the need for a new direction, which he means to seek through attempting a British epic. According to Anna Beer, 'Elegy for Damon' should be read 'as a crisis-driven exploration of poetry *and* sexuality.'[37] The poem confirms that, for Milton, classical allusion was the language of close friendship. We saw this even in relation to Thomas Young, a rather dour Scot. The playful posturing of invoking the Muses and so forth was how Milton let his hair down. The elegy, his last poem in Latin, is a goodbye not just to Charles but also to the form of literary fun they had together.

Even more important for his future life than the news of Charles' death was another sort of news from home – news of another Charles. A political crisis was brewing. He later claimed that he felt obliged to hurry home from Italy, to offer his services to the cause of English liberty, but that should not be taken very seriously. It was just time for him to go home, and his grasp of the domestic political outlook was probably sketchy.

What had happened in his absence is that Scotland had revolted against Charles and Laud. Their attempt to introduce a new Prayer Book that would bring Scottish worship into line with English had provoked the 'national covenant', a statement of Calvinist resistance. The Scottish bishops, seen as colonial stooges, fled south: Charles had lost control of his northern kingdom. Instead of negotiating, he was adamant that his authority, his very identity as monarch, depended on his right to determine religious policy. If the Scots were rejecting his Prayer Book and his bishops, they were rejecting him. The covenanters were traitors, he insisted. So he set about putting the rebellion down. But he proceeded

---

37   Beer 2008, p. 110.

ineptly, with a muddled invasion. To fund a more effective war he needed Parliament's help. But there were new fears among MPs that Charles had made a secret alliance with Spain, that a 'popish plot' was underway.

These developments confirmed Milton's sense that Charles's regime was a serious threat to English liberty. The king had failed to call Parliament since 1629, defying the unwritten rule that it should meet every few years: his 'personal rule' rejected the tradition that had emerged under Elizabeth and his father. By the late 1630s, MPs had begun to organize effective opposition: in 1637, Hampden and others objected to a new tax, 'ship money', as all taxes were meant to be approved by Parliament.

By sidelining Parliament the king had handed more power to the bishops, and they were making keen use of it. The Church had become a nervy, authoritarian institution, busily enforcing internal discipline: 'the Caroline Church differed from its predecessors in that it witnessed an unparalleled number of prosecutions in diocesan consistories, in particular over canonical disobedience.'[38] Writers of anti-ecclesiastical pamphlets were sometimes subjected to brutal punishments. In 1637, for example, three men had their ears cut off and their faces branded, on Laud's orders, for attacking bishops in print. And Charles had allowed the Church to reclaim certain rights, and certain lands, that it had lost since the Reformation – clerics were now regaining local political power. Milton had been half-aware of all this for a decade, but his sense of urgency was sharpened by the news that reached him in Italy: the heavy-handed policies of Charles and Laud had put violent enmity between England and Scotland.

To restore order Charles needed the help of Parliament, but the Parliament that assembled at the beginning of 1640 was hardly compliant. It was dominated by the very idea that had been forming in Milton's mind. Liberty was under threat, and must be urgently defended from an authoritarian clericalist regime. The Puritan MP John Pym demanded the abolition of church courts and the Star Chamber, and tougher action against Catholics. Charles angrily dissolved Parliament, and became more reliant than ever on Laud, and also on his wife's Catholic friends. In effect,

---

38   Davies 1992, p. 291.

Charles used the convocation of the bishops as an alternative parliament, passing new laws that tightened Church discipline, and extended ecclesiastical powers into secular areas. MPs had opposed such moves for years, but now their opposition was galvanized as never before. A new source of grievance was the oath that clergy now had to take, promising obedience to the king, his bishops, '. . . et cetera' – the vague ending seemed a sort of blank cheque of obedience. Maybe, some said, it was a prelude to the reintroduction of Roman Catholicism.

In November 1640, Charles was forced to call a new Parliament, known as the Long Parliament, which effectively launched a coup against him, by arresting his chief ministers, Strafford and Laud. There were to be another two years of limbo, before the first blood was shed in the civil war. Parliament demanded the right to dismantle Charles's regime, and determine religious policy. Pym and his friends were careful not to attack the king himself, but to blame his advisers. The Root and Branch Petition demanded the abolition of episcopacy; it led to a bill banning certain aspects of Laud's reforms, and effectively sanctioning iconoclasm. London opinion was now decidedly anticlerical: there were violent demonstrations against bishops as they took their seats in the Lords.

Milton, meanwhile, was starting a new life: he had taken new lodgings just off Fleet Street, where he was joined by his two nephews, whom he taught. He enjoyed teaching, and thinking about educational theory. He was soon to write a tract on the subject, in which he explained that the purpose of education 'is to know God.'[39] It should instil in boys 'high hopes of living to be brave men, and worthy Patriots, dear to God, and famous to all ages.'[40] All boys should be encouraged to be as idealistic as he was. They should want to improve the culture around them: the teaching of literature 'should make them soon perceive what despicable creatures our common Rimers and Playwriters be and show them what religious, what glorious and magnificent use, might be made of poetry both in divine and humane things.'[41]

---

39   Milton, *Of Education*, CPW vol. 2, p. 367.
40   Ibid., p. 385.
41   Ibid., p. 405.

Between marking their essays, he was entering the political fray. In the spring of 1641, he wrote his first pamphlet, 'Of Reformation in England, and the causes that have hitherto hindered it'. It was to be the first in a series of five anti-episcopal, or anti-prelatical, polemics (the word 'prelacy' refers to bishops and other senior clergy). Though he is writing to the present situation, his scope is wider than one might expect: he is also sketching a very radical theological position, which he is clearly developing as he goes. It is therefore quite wrong to see Milton's anti-episcopal writing as dustily irrelevant to us today. Of course anyone who reads them will discover that they are far from dusty: the prose is punchy and fresh. But who is interested in some old row from church history? But for Milton the question of episcopacy directly relates to the place of religion in society: should religion be tied to political power? Should an official form of religion be imposed by the state?

The conventional view is that Milton was now an enthusiastic Presbyterian (British Calvinist), and that he gradually extricated himself from the commitment a few years later. But actually he never shows many signs of subscribing to orthodox Calvinism. For the time being, he is willing to sound sympathetic to the movement, but it seems unlikely that he ever gave it his heart. Even in these first tracts a very personal form of Christian radicalism is sometimes evident. And it is clear that he was already reading the pamphlets of radical separatists such as Roger Williams, who taught that the church should retain a sort of anarchic looseness, with each congregation fully sovereign.

This first tract begins with the widest possible sketch of Christian history. The pure, spiritual gospel was subverted by the Catholic Church. Its priests 'began to draw down all the divine intercourse betwixt God and the soul, yea, the very shape of God himself, into an exterior and bodily form, urgently pretending a necessity and obligement of joining the body in a formal reverence and worship circumscribed . . .'[42] He seems to be attacking the very idea of the Church, as an institution that claims to mediate God through its ritual life. The priests, he goes on, insisted that this human institution was divine, and sought to make it duly seductive:

---

42   Milton, *Of Reformation*, CPW vol. 1, p. 520–1.

'. . . they hallowed it, they fumed up, they sprinkled it, they bedecked it, not in robes of pure innocency, but in robes of pure linen, with other deformed and fantastic dresses, in palls and mitres, gold, and gewgaws fetched from Aaron's old wardrobe, or the flamins' vestry . . .'[43] A 'gewgaw' is a trifle or bauble; a 'flamin' (usually spelled 'flamen') is a pagan priest. Catholicism is effectively a return to Judaism (and paganism): grand ritual is enforced by an authoritarian priesthood. The theatre of high church worship is accused of masking its violence.

The Gospel's purity was restored by 'the bright and blissful Reformation', which is sketched in very Foxean terms. It ended 'the black and settled night of ignorance and antichristian tyranny . . . shaking the powers of darkness and scorning the fiery rage of the old red dragon'.[44] Like Foxe, he credits England with sparking the Reformation – and yet something has gone very wrong. In terms of discipline, 'we are no better than a schism from all the Reformation'.[45] By insisting that bishops are necessary, the English Church implicitly denies the legitimacy of other Protestant churches; it resembles an imitation Rome. And now he turns on the actual episcopal regime that is clinging on to power. They are not true bishops, 'that have filled this land with late confusion and violence, but a tyrannical crew and corporation of impostors . . .'[46] True bishops, he explains, are chosen by 'the church assembled in convenient manner.' Soon he repeats the claim: 'bishops must be elected by the hands of the whole church.'[47] He cites Cyprian and other Church Fathers to this effect. The English Church by contrast has become anti-democratic: church interiors have been re-styled to aggrandize the priest and cow the laity into submission:

> The table of communion, now become a table of separation, stands like an exalted platform upon the brow of the quire, fortified with bulwark and barricade, to keep off the profane touch of the laics, whilst

---

43   Ibid., p. 521.
44   Ibid., p. 524–5.
45   Ibid., p. 526.
46   Ibid., p. 537.
47   Ibid., p. 541.

the obscene and surfeited priest scruples not to paw and mammoc the
sacramental bread as familiarly as his tavern biscuit.[48]

His hatred of the priest's touch is reminiscent of Hamlet's disgust at the
idea of his uncle fondling his mother. Indeed there is something Hamlet-
like throughout, in the alarmed awareness that the religious world is out
of joint. His rhetoric is of course iconoclastic: it wants to pull down the
aura of solemn glory that surrounds the Laudian liturgy. Here he focuses
on the altar-rail, an innovation that had actually been championed by
Charles himself. (In 1634, he had decreed that communion should be
received whilst kneeling at the altar-rail, that any variation on this was
unseemly. Laud had actually been rather nervous of the enforcement of
this symbolic division between priesthood and laity.)

The great crime of this crypto-Catholic church is to make the laity into
mere spectators: 'the people . . . give over the earnest study of virtue and
godliness, as a thing of greater purity than they need, and the search of
divine knowledge as a mystery too high for their capacities, and only
for churchmen to meddle with . . .'[49] This is exactly the complaint of
Luther, and of his chief English follower Tyndale. A genuinely popular
form of Christianity is made impossible by clericalism, for people see
priests as a separate class, and leave religion to them. Incidentally he
repeatedly cites Chaucer as a critic of a powerful Church: he sees himself
in a literary anticlerical tradition, in which lay writers have a valid claim
to authority.

So what does Milton want? It sounds as if he wants the Church to
become more democratic, more lay-run. So he wants a Church that has
been purified of worldliness. But of course that is no small thing to ask.
It means that in effect he wants the abolition of the Church as a politically
empowered institution. He now becomes more explicit about this, argu-
ing that the Constantinian revolution of the fourth century, that put the
Church at the heart of the state, was a mistake. It elevated the clergy 'from
a mean and plebian life on a sudden to be lords of stately palaces, rich

48   Ibid., p. 547–8.
49   Ibid., p. 548.

furniture, delicious fare, and princely attendance. . .'[50] There is an element of snobbery here: why should common types like Laud be catapulted to quasi-aristocratic status? It upsets the natural social order. More importantly, their power disrupts the body politic. Their courts undermine popular trust in the rule of law. It is worth noting that this questioning of Constantinianism, the idea that the Church should be politically empowered, goes beyond mainstream Protestant idealism. The English Reformation had of course been Constantinian, dependent on the monarch's willingness to empower true religion by means of an established Church. Milton signals his readiness to question this entire inheritance.[51]

Episcopacy has led to cultural decadence, to a subversion of proper manliness. As Anna Beer has recently argued, this is an important part of Milton's vision: he was always concerned with 'the restoration of English manliness'.[52] The prelates' aim has been 'to supple us either for a foreign invasion or domestic oppression . . . to despoil us both of manhood and grace . . .'[53] Of course it is already a Protestant trope, that Catholicism is louche, camp, queer, but Milton makes it his own: his anti-Catholicism seems to fuse with a half-conscious homophobia.

A key point he makes is that it is a fallacy to suppose that the monarch needs the bishops. In fact the authority of the crown is jeopardized by its association with them. 'Have [the bishops] not been bold of late to check the common law, to slight and brave the indiminishable majesty of our highest court, the lawgiving and sacred parliament? Do they not plainly labour to exempt churchmen from the magistrate?'[54] His point is that the secular law must be absolutely sovereign; there is no room for another form of legal authority that claims divine sanction, but is not accountable. If this is tolerated, then the body politic is unsettled; and the monarch risks forfeiting the trust of the people. Milton is demanding a clarification of politics, in a secularist direction. The state must not allow an

---

50 Ibid., p. 557.
51 Christopher Hill underlines the importance of this dissent from Constantine in Hill, *Milton and the English Revolution*, London: Faber 1977, p. 84–5.
52 Beer 2008, p. 168.
53 Milton, *Of Reformation*, Ibid., p. 588.
54 Ibid., p. 593–4.

unaccountable religious authority to take root. This position should be seen as a continuation, or updating, of the theory that underlies the English Reformation. As we saw in Chapter 1, the English Church adapted Luther's vision: the Church should be cut off from foreign control, and made into a department of state. It should become part of the national political unit. This is what happened under the Tudors. But something went wrong. The Church somehow held on to its autonomy. It became a national version of Roman Catholicism. It ought to have been fully secularized – deprived of power, made absolutely accountable to secular politics.

Milton attacks the bishops' aesthetic indulgence: by surrounding themselves with finery they hope their claim to authority will go unchallenged. But actually their theatrical apparel is ridiculous: why should 'the rustling of their silken cassocks' command respect? Why should not we laugh 'to see them under sail in all their lawn and sarcenet, their shrouds and tackle, with a geometrical rhomboids upon their heads'?[55] This is the verbal equivalent of a political cartoon: a sketch that punctures a public figure's claim to authority.

But now Milton switches from cartoonist to prophet: the tract climaxes in an audacious prayer. He reminds God that he did 'build up this Brittanic empire to a glorious and enviable height, with all her daughter-islands about her', and that he caused 'the northern ocean' to be strewn 'with the proud shipwrecks of the Spanish armada.'[56] And now, rather presumptuously, he tells God that a great deal more is expected: 'Hitherto thou hast but freed us, and that not fully, from the unjust and tyrannous claim of thy foes; now unite us entirely, and appropriate us to thyself, tie us everlastingly in willing homage to the prerogative of thy eternal throne.'[57] This is an astute bit of rhetoric, for he avoids the familiar idea that the nation became divinely chosen under Elizabeth. This would enable conservatives to point out that this golden age was episcopal. Instead, the nation has long been *on the cusp* of divine election. The

55   Ibid., p. 611–12.
56   Ibid., p. 614.
57   Ibid., p. 615.

alleged Elizabethan golden age was nothing to what is coming. Which is what? It can only be imagined in relation to the Second Coming. If the English empire can fully defeat Catholic reaction, it can expect

> to be found the soberest, wisest and most Christian people at that day, when thou, the eternal and shortly expected King, shalt open the clouds to judge the several kingdoms of the world, and distributing national honours and rewards to religious and just commonwealths, shalt put an end to all earthly tyrannies, proclaiming thy universal and mild monarchy through heaven and earth . . .[58]

This flirts with patriotic utopianism: when our church is purified, England will be a sort of landing-base for Christ's return.

What is exciting about this tract is Milton's determination to get to the heart of the matter – to cut through the crap that surrounds religious culture, the poncy flummery of it all. At one point he quotes the early church theologian Cyprian: religious custom should not be idolized, 'for custom without truth is but agedness of error.'[59] This could stand as his theological epitaph.

There were hundreds of political pamphlets, now that licensing had broken down. Milton obviously hoped that his would be immediately influential, but he also took a longer view, aware that it would be dusted down and read once he was famous, and his authorial development studied. He presented a copy to the Bodleian Library.

In the summer, he published another tract, *Of Prelatical Episcopacy*. It responded to two defences of episcopacy – by Joseph Hall, Bishop of Exeter, and James Ussher, Archbishop of Armagh. Episcopacy is a human tradition, Milton argues: there is no hint in the Bible that God ordains it as necessary. The nation is therefore free to choose whether or not to retain it. The early church fathers who founded the tradition of divine episcopacy, Ignatius and Irenaeus, are not beyond criticism (and the texts attributed to them may not be authentic). Their claim that the apostles

---

58   Ibid., p. 616.
59   Ibid., p. 561.

intended to found a higher rank of priest is unconvincing. Above all, we must reject the idea that these dubious texts have authority over us: if we dare not challenge them, 'then must we be constrained to take upon our selves a thousand superstitions, and falsities which the Papist will prove us down in from as good authorities, and as ancient, as these that set a Bishop above a Presbyter.'[60] The Protestant must not be intimidated by 'all the heaped names of Angels, and Martyrs, Councils, and Fathers urged upon us', nor by the 'Ephod and Teraphim of Antiquity'.[61] The latter words refer to the ornately bejeweled outfits worn by Israelite priests at a time when true worship was being forgotten. The image associates traditionalism with aestheticism, and accuses both of idolatry. Milton acknowledges that there is something impressive, including aesthetically impressive, about an appeal to ancient precedent. It takes guts to refuse to be charmed.

Another tract was published in July. It responded to a further work by Bishop Hall, in which he had defended himself against a team of Presbyterian writers who called themselves Smectymnuus, a name composed from five men's initials. The 'ty' belonged to Milton's former tutor Thomas Young. It seems that Milton was muscling in on someone else's dispute, in a bid to find a wider audience. He was trying to make a name for himself: though he was not yet putting his name to the tracts, he wanted his voice to be noticed, and traced to him. In this tract, known as *Animadversions*, he goes through Hall's text, replying at length to each point. He is particularly provoked by Hall's observation that previous generations of Englishmen had no problem with episcopacy, that it was not seen as an issue 'before this present age'. This is a strong point, for bishops such as Cranmer were among England's key reformers. Milton lets rip at the bishop's habitual conservatism: 'This was the plea of Judaism, and Idolatry against Christ and his Apostles, of Papacy against Reformation.' Hall has referred to 'this present age' with a hint of proto-Tory scorn: but 'it is to us an age of ages wherein God is manifestly come down among us, to do some remarkable good to our Church or state.' Hall writes 'as if a

---

60   Milton, *Of Prelatical Episcopacy*, CPW vol. 1, p. 651.
61   Ibid., p. 652.

man should tax the renovating and re-ingendring Spirit of God with innovation, and that new creature for an upstart novelty; yea the New Jerusalem, which without your admired link of succession descends from heaven, could not escape some such like censure.'[62] History is beginning to yield to the Second Coming: *of course* theology, and ecclesiology, is breaking with the past! And it is not surprising that this nation is the site of this millenarian novelty, for God 'hath yet ever had this Island under the special indulgent eye of his providence.'[63]

Ending episcopacy would imperil the honour due to the priesthood, Hall had said. But the true honour of Christian ministry lies in spreading God's word. 'Can a man thus employed find himself discontented, or dishonoured . . . because he may not as a Judge sit out the wrangling noise of litigious courts . . .?'[64] True Christian ministers are not meant to have political authority: simple as that.

It took a certain amount of courage to write so forcefully against the bishops, even anonymously, and even though the tide was turning against the bishops. It was still possible that Parliament's rebellion would be nipped in the bud, and these rabble-rousing writers tracked down. Milton was taking a risk, and enjoying it. At one point he responds to Hall's suggestion that anti-episcopal plotters ought to be punished: 'The punishing of that which you call our presumption and disobedience lies not now within the execution of your fangs, the merciful God above and our just Parliament will deliver us from your Ephesian beasts, your cruel Nimrods with whom we shall be ever fearless to encounter.'[65]

Parliament's power was indeed steadily increasing. In June 1641, it passed the 'Root and Branch' Bill abolishing episcopacy; in September, it abolished church courts. And in the following month the crisis sped up alarmingly: the Irish revolted, massacring their Protestant rulers. If England lost control of Ireland, it was highly vulnerable to Catholic invasion. But in the circumstances, Charles was not trusted to lead an army. So Parliament raised the stakes, and issued a new set of demands called

62   Milton, *Animadversions Upon the Remonstrants Defence against Smectymnuus*, ibid., p. 703.
63   Ibid., p. 704.
64   Ibid., p. 721–2.
65   Ibid., p. 729.

the Grand Remonstrance. Charles' response was to attempt a sort of counter-coup; he tried to have Pym, Hampden and three other MPs arrested. It was a PR disaster; it made him look like a nervy tyrant. Charles fled London, 'a little like a driver walking away from the scene of an accident.'[66] He went north, rallying his supporters. Parliament arrested thirteen bishops, and demanded the dismantling of episcopacy. How could Charles even meet such a demand half-way? His tactic was to dismiss his opponents as Calvinist fanatics. This forced moderates to choose between a stubborn king and his increasingly extreme opponents. Charles gambled, wrongly, that they would stick with the devil they knew. Instead the majority of MPs got off the fence and sided with the radicals.

Early in 1642, Milton must have felt rather powerful. His rhetoric had helped Parliament to stand up to the king (he doubtless felt this to be so, whether or not it was). He had cockily warned the bishops that the times were a-changing, and now they were behind bars. It must have felt very good. He now wrote his longest tract yet, and the first to be signed. And, to his future biographers' delight, he felt that his readers were probably keen to know something about this bold new voice, and about the grand vision that lay behind his polemics. As a consequence, *The Reason of Church Government* is one of the strangest polemical texts ever written.

It is much less aggressive than the previous tracts: it was now necessary to sound calm, constructive – more like a government spin-doctor than an opposition one. He begins by affirming the need for discipline, in religious as in secular life. He explains, following Luther, that the Gospel brings freedom from outward religious forms, and that it therefore has a minimalist concept of priesthood that eschews power and glory. The notion of a higher order of priest goes against this. Defenders of episcopacy point to the Old Testament, where there is a higher rank of priest. Imitating Judaism is retrograde, says Milton. They also say that episcopacy is needed to unite the church, that it will otherwise splinter apart. (This, incidentally, remains the key Anglican justification for it.[67]) In that case, replies Milton, why did not Paul insist on it, to keep the Corinthian

---

66   Carlton 1992, p. 234.
67   See my *Anarchy, Church and Utopia: Rowan Williams on Church*, London: DLT, 2003, *passim*.

church together? Maybe, he admits, the removal of episcopacy will bring more sects to light. But so what? This is a by-product of reformation: sects and schisms 'are but as the throws and pangs that go before the birth of reformation.'[68] Important new events are bound to be messy – just as the sculpting of a great marble statue strews the floor with splinters and chips. There is an important contradiction in Milton's thought: he claims that the church needs a new sort of discipline, that getting rid of bishops will make it more orderly; yet he also calls for a de-centralization of religious culture, and accepts this will make it more openly fragmented. His claim is that the fragmentation will be a temporary necessity.

The second part of this tract changes tack completely and reflects on the phenomenon of prophetic vocation. It considers the awkward position of a man who is called by God to say harsh things, offensive things. He must overcome his qualms, of course. Milton now drops the impersonality: if he ignored his sense of religious obligation, how could he subsequently live with himself? He imagines reproaching himself in later life:

> when time was, thou could not find a syllable of all that thou hast read, or studied, to utter in her [ie. the church's] behalf. Yet ease and leisure was given thee for thy retired thoughts, out of the sweat of other men. Thou hast the diligence, the parts, the language of a man, if a vain subject were to be adorned or beautified; but when the cause of God and his Church was to be pleaded . . . thou wert dumb as a beast.[69]

It is interesting that his unease about his financial dependence surfaces here. Because he has not provided for himself, he has especially little right to put convenience before duty. His intellectual and poetic identity is not of his own making: he does not own it. His financial dependence therefore blurs with his dependence on the will of God.

Why does he hesitate to get stuck in? This is not how he had intended to launch himself as a writer – as a religious polemicist. He had wanted to

---

68   Milton, *The Reason of Church Government*, CPW vol.1, p. 795.
69   Ibid., p. 804–5.

'take such a subject as of itself might catch applause, whereas this hath all the disadvantages on the contrary; and such a subject as the publishing whereof might be delayed at pleasure, and time enough to pencil it over with all the curious touches of art, even to the perfection of a faultless picture . . .'[70] He was meant to be an artist. He had dreamed of perfection of the work. Because his real authorial talents lie elsewhere, he is presently making use 'but of my left hand.'[71] It is strange to say this in the midst of a polemic. It is as if an MP were to begin his maiden speech, on a matter of great national urgency, by explaining that he was really an opera singer, that this politics business was not exactly what he was cut out for.

And now he offers a brief sketch of the poet behind the polemicist: his father nurtured his literary precocity, he has written some poems that pleased the Italians, and recently he has been gearing up to write the great English epic: 'what the greatest and choicest wits of Athens, Rome, or modern Italy, and those Hebrews of old did for their country, I in my proportion, with this over and above, of being a Christian, might do for mine. . .'[72] He now justifies this ambition in religious terms: a great national poet has a moral and religious function; his

> abilities . . . are of power, beside the office of a pulpit, to imbreed and cherish in a great people the seeds of virtue and public civility, to allay the perturbations of the mind, and set the affections in right tune; to celebrate in glorious and lofty hymns the throne and equipage of God's almightiness, and what he works, . . . to deplore the general relapses of kingdoms and states from justice and God's true worship.[73]

The last bit, as we shall see, is prophetic of the function of his epics. The poet should communicate 'whatsover in religion is holy and sublime' to his generation, make it attractive to them.[74] Literature is thus central to

---

70   Ibid., p. 807.
71   Ibid., p. 808.
72   Ibid., p. 812.
73   Ibid., p. 816–17.
74   Ibid., p. 817.

the health of the state, not the hobby of a few fops. This leads him to a wider reflection on the idea of national culture. Perhaps the state should follow classical precedent and organize the cultural life of the people – not by licensing drunken revels, as Charles' *Book of Sports* did, but by establishing universal military training, and open universities. The teaching of wisdom and virtue should be culturally central: 'Whether this may not be, not only in pulpits, but after another persuasive method, at set and solemn paneguries, in theatres, porches, or what other place or way may win most upon the people to receive at once both recreation and instruction, let them in authority consult.'[75]

Here is a new aspect of Milton's vision: the nation whose religion is fully integrated into its cultural life, its popular cultural life. The radicalism of this can hardly be overstated. Most obviously he anticipates Hegel, who also saw Greek culture as a model of organic unity, in which religion and culture were one. Milton perceives that Christianity, in its traditional forms, gets in the way of this cultural ideal; it looks down on ordinary, secular cultural life. He is reviving the humanist idealization of secular culture, but from an authentically Christian perspective that follows Luther's affirmation of the secular. Religion must find full expression in 'the arts'. He has already said that the poet's 'abilities . . . are of power, beside the office of a pulpit', to communicate true religion. And now the same idea: it is 'not only in pulpits' that religion must be affirmed. It must break out of its old subculture and be culturally dispersed. We must learn from the 'total' culture of ancient Athens: their religion was expressed in huge, popular cultic events ('paneguries'). We need a new sort of reformation in which the Gospel permeates all aspects of culture. England's new theatrical life can play a role here: 'porches' refers to the medieval tradition of religious theatre, that gave rise to the Mystery Play tradition. The key point is that religion ought to be truly pan-cultural, not confined to a strange subculture called church. He has a dream – of being the national poet who sparks this cultural revolution, which is the joint climax of the Renaissance and the Reformation. It will revive the spirit of

75   Ibid., p. 819–20.

ancient Athens, not for pagan reasons but because the Reformation calls for a truly cultural revolution, Christianity's unfolding into an authentically socio-political expression.

So this is his vision, he tells his readers. He wants to help create this new order. And instead he has to argue with bigoted pedants – 'to club quotations with men whose learning and belief lies in marginal stuffings.'[76] Milton was unusual in rejecting the convention of cramming his margins with notes intended to bolster the authority of the text – the implication was that his words had intrinsic authority and did not need such small-print aid. But the main point he is making is that he has had to lower himself, to trade insults with the footnote brigade, in order to refute the defenders of episcopacy. He has to play the role of bullish theologian. But on what authority does he enter this religious dispute? If he really cares about the church, why is not he a priest? Why should an outsider, who seems more interested in poetry than religion, be allowed to hold forth on church politics? I am no outsider to the church, Milton insists,

> to whose service, by the intentions of my parents and friends, I was destined of a child, and in mine own resolutions: till coming to some maturity of years and perceiving what tyranny had invaded the Church, that he who would take orders must subscribe slave, and take an oath withal, which unless he took with a conscience that would retch, he must either straight perjure, or split his faith, I thought it better to prefer a blameless silence before the sacred office of speaking bought, and begun with servitude and forswearing. Howsoever thus Church-outed by the Prelates, hence may appear the right I have to meddle in these matters . . .[77]

This is a rhetorical sequel to Luther's 'Here I stand, I can do no other.' The Church being tainted, one is called to an extra-ecclesial prophetic standpoint. This will be seen as arrogance by those who fail to understand its necessity – so be it.

---

76   Ibid., p. 822.
77   Ibid., p. 822–3.

A few months later he wrote his final anti-prelatical tract, whose long title is normally shortened to *An Apology for Smectymnuus*. It responds to an attack on his previous pamphlets. He is responding to an attempted character assassination, and enjoys the opportunity to talk about himself. No, he was not thrown out of university, or barred from ordination – he was certainly not the moral inferior of those who went on to be ordained. He cannot resist a quick snipe at the low calibre of the ordinands he encountered. They were a bunch of hearty idiots, Tim-Nice-But-Dims: he recalls them performing some amateur dramatics, and winces, eloquently. This passage is often cited as evidence of Milton's mean-mindedness and pride. But it is no nastier than the witty put-downs that the contemporary columnist produces twice a week. And having been personally attacked, Milton at least has some excuse.

No, he is not some sort of libertine who haunts playhouses and dodgy nightclubs, he tells his accuser. And let us be absolutely clear about this, he says: I have never used prostitutes. Most people would deny such a charge very swiftly, and move on. But Milton wants to talk about his sex life, or lack of it. Chastity is absolutely central to his inner life, he asserts. He has always idealized virginity, in the chivalric tradition of courtly love. What drew him to the poetry of Dante and Petrarch was not louche aestheticism but the moral idealism he found there. And he began to feel 'that he who would not be frustrate of his hope to write well hereafter in laudable things, ought himself to be a true poem, that is, a composition and pattern of the best and honourablest things . . .'[78] And he was also saved from sexual temptation by 'a certain niceness of nature, an honest haughtiness, and self-esteem either of what I was, or what I might be (which let envy call pride).'[79] There is no passage that is so liable to make Milton's worldly detractors splutter into their sherry. How dare he talk about his virginity as if it is a badge of righteousness. 'What a prig!' shrieks Rowse: 'Moral virtue has nothing to do with artistic achievement: look at Byron or Baudelaire, Dickens or Balzac or Proust, or for that matter

---

78   Ibid., p. 890.
79   Ibid.

Shakespeare or Marlowe.'[80] It is Rowse who is dogmatic, insisting on the amorality of art: for Milton it is not so; his idea of poetic creation is founded on a deeply moral sensibility. Fine, some would say, but he ought to keep this quiet, instead of drawing attention to his physical and spiritual purity. But the context justifies it. He has been vaguely accused of libertinism, of being an untrustworthy flâneur: you know what these literary types are like, his accuser is saying – why should we let such a character lecture us on religion? Milton knows that he is vulnerable to such insinuations, being detached from the Church. His defiant assertion of purity might be a bit embarrassing for us worldly moderns to hear, but it is undeniably effective: it kills off the libertine image forever. He removes any ambiguity from his poetic identity: he has never had anything in common with the free-wheeling young-Donne type. He is a sort of parapriest, unordained yet dedicated.

Once it returns to politics, the tract turns into a rapt eulogy for Parliament. It has stood up to episcopacy, in the name of liberty. The MPs' resolve, in facing down the Church, has been miraculous. Against the odds they have heroically served 'religion and their native liberty. Which two things God hath inseparably knit together, and hath disclosed to us, that they who seek to corrupt our religion, are the same that would enthrall our civil liberty.'[81] Parliament has in a sense replaced the Church, as the prime agent of God's will.

The final part of the tract addresses the question of religious propriety, in relation both to worship and pamphleteering rhetoric. Milton's opponent has rebuked him for mixing polemic with prayer, thus demeaning the sanctity of prayer. He seems angry 'to find any prayers but in the service book', Milton replies. 'It was theatrical, he says. And yet it consisted most of scripture language: it had no rubric to be sung in an antique cope upon the stage of a high altar.'[82] This is a good example of Milton's determination to attack the air of sombre pomp that attaches to high Church tradition. Why should a rigid institutional setting make a prayer

---

80   Rowse 1977, p. 60.
81   Ibid., p. 923–4.
82   Ibid., p. 930.

authentic? Why should not prayer be free, deregulated? Christian rhetoric ought to be dispersed through culture, including political pamphlets, rather than confined to Church services. God wills to be proclaimed more generally, and more freely.

He goes on to insist that the Prayer Book must be pulled from its pedestal, for it is far too close to Rome. It is idolatrous to prefer 'decency' in worship to theological truth. This conservative-aesthetic habit is a subtle form of captivity to Rome's influence – and here he offers an astute analogy. It is as if the English Church has got divorced from the Roman harlot, but has been foolish enough to hang on to a few of her things, for old time's sake. Through these keepsakes she continues to exert her dark charm on us: 'For we are deep in dotage.'[83] This is a brilliant analysis of the English Reformation: the old religion remains firmly under the skin; we are in thrall to it. Milton is urging his compatriots to an act of ecclesial exorcism: we must get over her, get her out of our system, move on.

The image has a misogynistic edge, of course: we must achieve clarity by rejecting evil female cunning. The idea of Rome as a whore is not Milton's invention, but he uses it with relish. And it will feature highly in his epics, especially *Samson Agonistes*. Does his attraction to such imagery suggest a pathological fear of female sexuality? It suggests a wider fear of being seduced. The prime object of this fear is aestheticism: being so impressed by beauty, order, dignity, majesty and antiquity that one's theological judgment is clouded. Milton sees serious, subtle demonic agency here, the sort that a religious-minded artist and intellectual is prone to. The seductive possibilities of actual women seem to trouble him far less. But he was about to encounter a form of sexual and emotional angst that he had not anticipated.

---

83   Ibid., p. 942.

4

The Idea of a Free Christian Society

He got married just as the war kicked off, in the summer of 1642, and it quickly went wrong. Mary Powell was the sixteen-year-old daughter of one of his father's business associates, who lived near Oxford. On a trip to the area, Milton decided to renew his acquaintance with the family. Nothing is really known about the courtship, except its haste. Maybe he was too keen to marry: maybe his new career as a political thinker had given him a new virile identity; he was a man of action almost, not an unworldly youth, and such a man needed a wife. So, after a month in the country, he returned to London with a young wife, to the amazement of his nephew-pupils. Nor is it known what went wrong. It seems likely that Milton found it hard to climb down from the proud pedestal of his virginity, to translate his intellectual confidence into sexual confidence. Such a sudden transition from an asexual to a sexual identity threw him, and he probably expressed his discombobulation in moody introversion. To borrow the opening of a recent Ian McEwan novel, '[t]hey lived in a time when a conversation about sexual difficulties was plainly impossible. But it is never easy.'[84] Or maybe the sex was fine, but they had nothing else in common: we do not know. What we know is that instead of trying to muddle through this early marital problem, Mary went home to her parents after just a month. It was meant to be a quick visit, but it was

---

84   Ian McEwan, *On Chesil Beach*, London: Cape, 2006, p. 1.

extended. The rising chaos of the war was a factor: her parents probably told her she was safer out of London, and she went along with this. Her parents' political conservatism added to this: they wanted their daughter on the royalist side of the battle line.

He was alone again, but for his nephews – the solitary poet, surrounded by war. In the autumn, the royalist forces came close to London, and he wrote a sonnet acknowledging his vulnerability, and restating his high poetic identity. It poses as a notice pinned to his door, addressing whatever military chief takes control of the area, asking him to protect this house and its owner, 'for he [ie. Milton] knows the charms / That call fame on such gentle acts as these, / And he can spread thy name o'er lands and seas . . .'. He presents himself as a sort of urban magician, whose artistic power ought to protect him from a grim random death in a war-zone. It shows that his lofty, romantic self-understanding has not been affected by his prose work.

Unsurprisingly he brooded on his failed marriage. He was furious with the Powell family: they had betrayed him. Marriage entails breaking away from one's family, seeing authority in one's spouse rather than one's parents, and they had made this impossible for her to do. The injustice of it appalled him. Through no fault of his own (as it seemed to him) he was legally bound, for life, to a woman who had betrayed his trust. Did he have to revert to an asexual identity, for life, just because her meddling family had sabotaged the marriage? In cases such as his, the finality of marriage was a nightmarish burden. If a marriage failed, the parties should be allowed to move on, have another chance of finding happiness. Of course we take this for granted now; it is a basic part of a free society. Milton's forensic mind turned to the politics of marriage. He started researching the issue, seeking evidence for his hunch that the idea of the indissolubility of marriage is a harmful taboo. In fact, it seems that his interest was not entirely prompted by his own circumstances: we know that he made notes on the subject before marrying.

He was taking a step back from religious politics, just as it was getting crucial. He was rethinking his religious identity. Up to now, he seemed, from a slight distance, to be a Presbyterian thinker. As we have seen, he was keen to seem a serious Puritan, not a flakey libertine poet – and so,

partly because of his acquaintance with Young, he sided with Smectymn-
uus. But now the landscape was changing. It was looking increasingly
likely that the Church of England would be replaced by a Presbyterian
system, as in Scotland. As the war got underway, Parliament formed an
alliance with the Scots: England's new religious order would be on the
Presbyterian model. Is this what Milton had been advocating the past
two years? He had evaded the question. What he had campaigned for
was negative: the removal of the old unaccountable episcopal order.
He had talked only very vaguely about the new order, about how the
Reformation would be completed. He hoped for a new pure Church that
no longer sought political power, and he observed that it would have to
be democratic: congregations would choose their leaders. But would
there have to be one central structure? Would the new Church have to be
in some sense official, and established? Would Parliament have to enforce
uniformity, orthodoxy? Instead of really addressing all this, he implied
that he was sympathetic to the Presbyterian project, through echoing
much of their rhetoric. In *The Reason of Church Government* he had said
that church discipline was 'beyond the faculty of man to frame, and . . .
dangerous to be left to man's invention.'[85] But how would this divine
society take shape? How would it triumph over heretical versions of
itself? Young and the other Smectymnuans took it for granted that an
orderly new church would take control, and keep heresy in check. Some
keen Scots, such as Robert Baillie, had come to London, to help bring this
about. Milton now asked himself if this is what he wanted: a bunch of zeal-
ous Scots in charge. Some MPs, including Lord Falkland, had expressed
their doubts about such a prospect. It was only now that Milton saw their
point – just as the Calvinists were taking control of the new religious
legislative body that was being created, the Westminster Assembly.

Instead of suddenly writing against the Puritans he had so recently
allied himself with, he changed the subject. He decided to publish his
thoughts on the marriage issue. Domestic liberty is an important part of
liberty, he announces. The personal is political. The reform of divorce law

---

85   Milton, *Of Reformation*, CPW vol. 1, p. 750.

is a priority. This was an eccentric announcement, a bit like an intellectual during the Second World War saying that a crucial aspect of the fight against fascism is the need to de-criminalize homosexuality. And of course strict Puritans were hostile: national morals need to be protected at this time of crisis, and re-thinking the meaning of marriage is not helpful, to put it mildly. One imagines the dismay of his old tutor Thomas Young: just when it seemed that his brilliant pupil had finally joined the Presbyterian cause, he comes out with this. By ignoring such people's opinion, Milton was signaling his detachment from the emerging new religious order.

His decision to publish on divorce is one of the most crucial of his career. It reflects his understanding that his true allegiance is not with the religious radicals who were gaining power, but with a more liberal tradition. Though he has proved his fluency in mainstream Puritan rhetoric, he must take a step back and question his religious and political agenda. He returns to Grotius' magnum opus, *De Jure Belli ac Pacis*, published in 1625, one of the most important attempts to sketch the principles of liberal society before the advent of Locke (Grotius is cited ten times in the first divorce tract). And he is also influenced by an English follower of Grotius, John Selden, a radical MP who had applied natural law theory to the Puritan cause. The point is that Milton's intellectual allegiance was wide: it took account of England's early tradition of rationalist sceptics, such as John Hales and Sir Henry Wotton (who had given him a letter of introduction to Grotius). At this point in his career Milton made the important decision not to cut off this freethinking source of influence, in order to make it as a Presbyterian writer. The forthcoming English revolution had to be open to all authentic enlightenment.

He was also alert to a new style of militant preaching that emphasized the need to fight for liberty above all else. Of course mainstream Puritan preachers such as William Prynne were cheering on Parliament, but there was also a new breed, a bit detached from Calvinism, known as 'Independents'. John Goodwin was the best known of these religious advisers to the radical MPs and generals. And, further to the left, John Lilburne was also gathering a following – he would go on to found the Levellers, the first democratic movement. Over the last few years Prynne

impose itself on a culture, and silence the opposition? That is to malign Christian tradition, Milton insists. Paul sometimes quoted pagan Greek writers, as did the church fathers. One of them, Dionysius Alexandrinus, wondered whether he ought to read pagan literature, and was told by God in a vision not to worry, for he would retain the power to judge the moral worth of such literature, rather than be corrupted by it. And he recalled Paul's dictum, 'Prove [ie. try] all things, hold fast to that which is good.' Milton backs this up with another Pauline saying: 'To the pure all things are pure.'[93] Not only are bad books powerless to hurt one: they can be good for one, by showing what one is up against. God does not want to keep the reader 'under a perpetual childhood of prescription'; he trusts him to develop critical faculties.[94] Citing the parable of the wheat and the tares, Milton insists that good and evil are so intermingled that it is folly to seek their neat separation. We must learn virtue in the midst of the mix: 'Assuredly we bring not innocence into the world, we bring impurity much rather: that which purifies us is trial, and trial is by what is contrary.'[95] And here he hails Spenser as 'a better teacher than Scotus or Aquinas': his epic shows how real virtue is formed by engaging with evil.

The attempt to separate 'safe' from 'harmful' literature is absurd: the Bible itself contains potentially corrupting material. And the urge to regulate would spread to all forms of culture, leading to the banning of music and dancing: every home would have to be spied on, to check that no one is playing excessively suggestive tunes on the lute or guitar. There is no sane alternative to allowing people to pursue their pleasures, in freedom. 'Wherefore did [God] create passions within us, pleasures round about us, but that these rightly tempered are the very ingredients of virtue?'[96] We must be free to make to mistakes, to abuse our freedom.

If intellectual freedom is restricted, 'what advantage is it to be a man over it is to be a boy at school . . .?'[97] 'And how can a man teach with authority, which is the life of teaching, how can he be a Doctor in his

---

93   Milton, *Areopagitica*, CPW vol. 2, p. 512.
94   Ibid., p. 514.
95   Ibid., p. 515.
96   Ibid., p. 527.
97   Ibid., p. 531.

book as he ought to be . . .?'[98] Here Milton uses his Italian experience: he
has seen how miserable life is on the other side of Rome's iron curtain,
how English liberty is envied. Let us make our culture truly worthy of
emulation, he says, by putting liberty at the very heart of our revolution.
Otherwise, those who were recently silenced from preaching 'shall come
now to silence us from reading, except what they please', and it will be
clear 'that Bishops and Presbyters are the same to us, both name and
thing.'[99] This is no time for such nervousness:

> While things are not yet constituted in Religion, that freedom of writ-
> ing should be restrained by a discipline imitated from the Prelates, and
> leaned by them from the Inquisition to shut us up all again into the
> breast of a licenser, must needs give cause of doubt and discourage-
> ment to all learned and religious men.[100]

It is precisely now, when religious culture is up in the air, that liberty must
be defended and a new orthodoxy resisted. Otherwise the new regime
will mirror the old. This insight is later to form the punchline to his son-
net: 'New Presbyter is but old Priest writ large.' This is the first time that
Milton has likened presbyters to bishops and it is perhaps the first time in
intellectual history that this famous dynamic of revolutions turning
repressive has been identified. *Animal Farm* is planted here.

The greater the regulation of religion, Milton argues, the less popular
engagement with religion there will be. Religion will seem too dangerous
for normal people to handle, better left to the priestly experts. If religious
culture is to thrive there must be a sense of popular ownership. (The
history of American religion is good evidence for this claim.) Excessive
regulation will also create an enfeebled priesthood, who never learn to
think for themselves. And culture as a whole will cut itself off from new
insights, 'little differing from that policy wherewith the Turk upholds his
Alcoran [ie. Koran], by the prohibition of printing.'[101]

---

98   Ibid., p. 532–3.
99   Ibid., p. 539.
100   Ibid., p. 541.
101   Ibid., p. 548.

Milton now warns against a simple, unitive concept of truth. Truth has been scattered throughout the world, like the dismembered victim Osiris. Truth will not be fully reconstructed until the Second Coming. Yet we must continue to seek, as Isis sought the scattered limbs of Osiris. In other words, truth is an endless project, not a stable possession. Protestants are in danger of forgetting this: 'We boast our light; but if we look not wisely on the sun itself, it smites us into darkness . . . The light which we have gained, was given us not to be ever staring on, but by it to discover onward things more remote from our knowledge.'[102] We cannot rely on some simple 'Reformation' blueprint to

> make us a happy nation. No, if other things as great in the Church, and in the rule of life both economical and political be not looked into and reformed, we have looked so long upon the blaze that Zwingli and Calvin hath beaconed up to us, that we are stark blind.[103]

Protestants who denounce sectarians and heretics, who nervously defend some new orthodoxy, are motivated not by love of truth but by 'their own pride and ignorance . . . They are the troublers, they are the dividers of unity, who neglect and permit not others to unite those dissevered pieces which are yet wanting to the body of Truth.'[104] This is the most explicit statement yet of his theological radicalism. The Reformation cannot be treated as a new orthodoxy, without betraying it. For new insights have arisen since the time of Zwingli and Calvin, principally in relation to politics. We are called to unite the body of Truth in new ways. And, Milton now goes on, the English have a special role to play. It is we who started the ball rolling, with Wycliffe, and it is back in our court:

> Now once again by all concurrence of signs, and by the general instinct of holy and devout men, as they daily and solemnly express their thoughts, God is decreeing to begin some new and great period in his

---

102   Ibid., p. 550.
103   Ibid.
104   Ibid., p. 550–1.

Church, even to the reforming of Reformation itself. What does he then but reveal himself to his servants, and as his manner is, first to his Englishmen?[105]

Instead of scoffing at such religious patriotism, we should acknowledge the boldness of Milton's vision here. He is trying to announce a new, liberal direction within Protestantism, and he is reading English history in such a way as to authorize this, to make it seem sure and strong. In England, he says, reformation has always been closely linked to the emergence of a more liberal polity. There is *some* truth in this. As we saw in Chapter 1, England's reformation was unusually open to the insights of humanism; and the idea of a reformed national church was tied up (however untidily) with a new sort of liberal polity. It makes sense that it should be here that the Reformation ditches its narrowness, discovers its full affinity with political enlightenment, with what we now know as 'liberalism', says Milton. Milton's genius is to see that this new level of reformation is precarious, due to the innate conservatism of religious leaders (look at the reactionary turn that Holland took in 1618). It needs to overlap with revolutionary patriotism. And so he returns to the patriotic-utopian rhetoric that we noted a few years earlier, but now with a clearer sense of what exact cause it is for: not Puritanism in general but explicitly liberal Puritanism.

The Presbyterians who cling to Calvinist dogma fail to see that God is drawing up new plans: 'He who hears what praying there is for light and clearer knowledge to be sent down among us, would think of other matters to be constituted beyond the discipline of Geneva, framed and fabricked already to our hands.'[106] It is cowardice to fetishise a hundred-year-old model, when a new religious and political era is unfolding. The way forward is Paul's principle that believers should choose for themselves what to eat, and more generally what rules to follow: 'How many other things may be tolerated in peace, and left to conscience, had we but charity, and were it not the chief stronghold of our hypocrisy to be ever

---

105   Ibid., p. 553.
106   Ibid., p. 561–2.

judging one another.'[107] We have been damaged by our submission to prelacy, he suggests, brutalized into wanting to imitate the old order that abused us. We have inherited, from our oppressors, a fear of 'heresy', of otherness. If we try to stamp out strange new styles of Christianity, that might contain crucial new insights, 'woe to us, while, thinking thus to defend the Gospel, we are found the persecutors.'[108] Here Milton is thinking of the new sects that have emerged in recent years, some of them shockingly odd.

Just before the publication of this pamphlet, Parliament had won a major victory at Marston Moor. Not only was this good news for the obvious reason, that it made a full and final victory for Parliament seem imminent; it also heralded the rise of a benign political movement. Thanks to its general, Oliver Cromwell, the army was becoming a counterweight to Presbyterianism. Cromwell and many other officers were Independents; Protestants who emphasized toleration, and saw Calvinism as dangerously narrow. It was a stroke of amazingly good fortune for Milton, that this rising military force was full of ideas remarkably close to his own.

Cromwell was a gentleman farmer, steeped in Puritanism since youth. He was irascible and melancholy by temperament; around 1630, he had a conversion experience, which brought a profound sense of calling. His hatred for Laudianism was so strong that he considered emigrating to the New World. (In a sense, he helped to invent America by staying at home, as did Milton.) Though he had never been a soldier he discovered a gift for organising troops and marshaling their vague zeal. He chose men of strong faith to serve under him; his army began to resemble a sort of church. Yet his faith-based leadership was inclusive rather than narrow; his genius was to create a big tent, a wide sense of religious purpose. He can only be understood if his extraordinary faith is acknowledged. He believed that God was in control of the strange events of the day. And, like Milton, he had a horror of legalism; his zeal was passionately anti-dogmatic. It is ironic that he is often mistaken for a hardline

---

107   Ibid., p. 563.
108   Ibid., p. 568.

Calvinist, for he saw Presbyterianism as little better than Laudianism; an alternative tyranny. He was sharply critical of the Presbyterian Scots he fought alongside: 'In the way they carry themselves now . . . I would as soon draw my sword against them as any in the King's army.'[109] He began to see himself as the protector of liberty: the new regime, he said, would have to respect 'tender consciences, who cannot in all things submit to the common rule which shall be established.'[110] No form of Protestantism should be banned, as long as it was no threat to peace. After the war he told Parliament: 'I had rather Mahometanism were permitted amongst us than that one of God's children should be persecuted.'[111] This immediately became a famous soundbite among his supporters, such as Milton, who prized liberty of conscience. Like Milton he thought Catholicism intolerable. As he said in 1649, 'if by liberty of conscience you mean a liberty to exercise the Mass, I . . . let you know, where the Parliament of England have power, that will not be allowed of.'[112] Yet (except in Ireland) he had no interest in actively persecuting those who were quietly Catholic.

So what religious settlement was he fighting for? He admitted that he did not exactly know. At the beginning of the war he had told some colleagues: 'I can tell you, Sirs, what I would not have; tho' I cannot, what I would.'[113] What was the actual alternative to an established episcopal Church? God knew, and should be trusted to provide it. The duty of good Christians was to defend true religion and liberty, whatever the consequences. Surely it is dangerous folly to pull down a political and religious order, with no clear sense of what to replace it with? Cromwell would reply (perhaps) that God called Abraham, and Moses, and all of Israel, they knew not where. England too was required to walk by faith in these exceptional times. He makes Tony Blair look like an agnostic.

---

109   Quoted in Antonia Fraser, *Cromwell: Our Chief of Men,* London: Phoenix Press (1973), 2000, p. 135.
110   Ibid., p. 136.
111   Ibid., p. 403.
112   Ibid., p. 347.
113   Ibid., p. 81.

So although he was depressed by the new Presbyterian order, Milton had grounds for hope: the army seemed intent on keeping it in check, and restoring the cause of liberty. He had other grounds for optimism. His painful marital situation was resolved, with the surprising return of his estranged wife in the summer of 1645. The resumed marriage was doubtless intensely difficult at first, but life went on, and soon Mary was pregnant. He had also taken on some more pupils, so they all moved to a larger house (his father now lived with him too). He was finally making his way in the world, aged thirty-seven, making a name for himself, starting a family. And as if to mark this transition he produced an edition of his poems, containing nearly all that he had written so far. He was keen to show how he had developed, how he had developed away from the effete aestheticism of the early elegies. One elegy is given a disclaimer, claiming to regret 'the trifling memorials of my levity which, with a warped mind and a base spirit, I once raised'. As usual he (rightly) thinks we are interested in his psychological development, the progress of his soul.

Having cleared the poetic decks, he started working on his long-term goal, and made the first attempts at *Paradise Lost*, which he first conceived as a drama. But political concerns would keep him from fully focusing on that project for another fifteen years.

Just as he was settling down to some domestic order, in 1646, the least desirable refugees knocked on his door: his in-laws, who had ruined the first years of his marriage. Parliamentary forces had seized their Oxfordshire estate. Some of their five other children probably came too. Milton swallowed his grudge against the family and took them in, which seems remarkably good of him. Perhaps he relished a chance to show his wife the meaning of marital duty. Added to this invasion, his daughter was seriously ill, and never fully recovered – it seems that she was both mentally and physically handicapped.

Was he happy in the midst of this extended family? Not very. We know from a letter that he wrote to one of his Italian friends that he felt lonely amid his noisy household, and stressed by the lingering war. He still did not quite belong to any intellectual community in England, and still looked back on his Italian gap-year as the time he was happiest.

Incidentally, his life at this stage might have been a lot happier had the internet been invented, allowing him to email his international Protestant-humanist network.

And another piece of modern technology would also have changed his life: eye-surgery. It was now that he realized there was something wrong with his eyesight. Reading had often given him pain over the last year or so. Over the next six years he gradually went blind.

His role was to keep on advertising liberty, in the teeth of the Presbyterian structures that were emerging. In 1646, Parliament approved a Presbyterian blueprint for the Church, and in response Milton wrote his most political sonnet yet, devoid of pretty pagan touches. 'On the New Forcers of Conscience Under the Long Parliament' accuses the Presbyterians of imitating their old foes, 'whose sin ye envied, not abhorred.' Under this Calvinist Taliban,

> . . . Men whose life, learning, faith, and pure intent
> Would have been held in high esteem with Paul
> Must now be named and printed heretics
> By shallow Edwards and Scotch what-d'ye-call!
> But we do hope to find out all your tricks,
> Your plots and packing, worse than those of Trent,
> That so the parliament
> May with their wholesome and preventive shears
> Clip your phylacteries, though balk [spare] your ears,
> And succour our just fears,
> When they shall read this clearly in your charge:
> New Presbyter is but old Priest writ large.

His poetic voice has a new public character: it is not the lone poet, but 'we', the liberty-loving Independents, who will hold them to account, through the firm but fair agency of Parliament. 'Phylacteries' are amulets containing Mosaic texts, worn by the Pharisees: Jesus criticizes the ostentatious piety (Matthew 23:5). 'Edwards' is Thomas Edwards, a Presbyterian pundit who had accused Milton's divorce tract of undermining family values, lumping its author with advocates of free-love. Parliament will deprive these new Pharisees of power, but will not mutilate their ears (the fate of some Puritans under Laud). Instead of vengeful violence, Parliament will restore order through a calm, authoritative statement, an unmasking of the new religious tyrants. Milton uses poetry to anticipate the power that he hopes will arise. And this is a key factor in his mature style: the calm authority of his voice is a token of the calm authority that the new liberal state must assume. It must trust in its religious authority, as Milton trusts in his.

The war ought to have ended in 1645, following Laud's execution and Cromwell's decisive victory at Naseby. But Parliament lost momentum, and the search for a new settlement was long and chaotic. The king was now the prisoner of the Presbyterian Scots, who offered him an unlikely deal: he could return to the throne if he let the English Church become Presbyterian. Many in Parliament were sympathetic to this. Charles played for time, expecting this internally divided revolution to collapse, and to be fully restored. Despite his defeat he was still in quite a strong position, while Parliament was so divided. But in May 1646, he fell out with the Scots, who allowed him to fall into the hands of Parliament. Under house arrest he remained bullish, refusing to accept the abolition of episcopacy: he pointed to the Magna Carta, which said that the king had a duty to defend the rights of the Church. He now entered martyr-mode. Had he not been betrayed by the Scots as Christ was by Judas, and handed to his enemies? He developed a new popular touch, befriending the servants with whom he was imprisoned. And his fastidious piety intensified; according to Clarendon, he 'was so severe an exactor of gravity and reverence in all mention of religion that he could never endure any light or profane word in religion.'[114]

Meanwhile Cromwell's army was emerging as a political force, the party of 'liberty'. It contained various types of radical, including Levellers who sought the radical redistribution of wealth, and universal suffrage. Cromwell somehow ordered this body, as ideologically unstable as a student union, and nurtured its identity as the true defender of liberty, the

---

114 Edward Hyde, Earl of Clarendon, *The History of the Great Rebellion*, ed. by Roger Lockyer, Oxford: Oxford University Press 1967, p. 456.

opponent of Presbyterian as well as royalist tyranny. The army held a wide-ranging conference at Putney in 1647 where the limits of toleration were discussed, as was the practicability of the Leveller vision. Cromwell came out with many impassioned pleas that the various progressive forces should work together, be patient, and trust God, for the sake of liberty. He kept the Levellers onside, with vague promises that he shared their agenda. The frank, excited idealism of the speeches recorded at Putney is remarkable: it is almost axiomatic that God is directing the English revolution, bringing entirely new political possibilities, something resembling a new heaven and a new earth.

This party conference, preparing for government, was premature: in 1648, royalist risings broke out, and the civil war re-ignited like a bonfire thought to have been extinguished. Milton was sick of the violent delay, impatient for a strong new regime to arrive, establishing liberty at last. He expressed this in a sonnet in praise of Fairfax, who had put down one of the new royalist risings. 'Fairfax, whose name in arms through Europe rings . . .' It's a poetic triumph: a poetic version of the Roman victory celebration. Through celebrating his military prowess, Milton urges him to a new political role. His warring has been heroic, but the real heroism will be his contribution to a new order, free of violence, corruption, greed.

Milton's scanty writing at this chaotic time includes his translation of some of the Psalms. The exercise reminded him that the Christian vision is rooted in absolute dependence on the authority of God, trust in his power to bring peace and order, on both a personal and a social level. The Psalms are a crucial key to understanding Milton's mind. Again and again, they juxtapose God's power and human weakness. The experience of humiliation and isolation is not shunned as embarrassing weakness, but put centre-stage, for it is through having our pride trashed that we learn to be dependent on God. The surprising fact is that God's strength corresponds not to human strength but to human vulnerability, to the psychological honesty born of suffering. Here, for example, is some of Milton's translation of Psalm 88: 'I am a man, but weak, alas, / And for that name unfit, / From life discharged and parted quite, / Among the dead to sleep . . . Why wilt thou, Lord, my soul forsake / And hide thy face from me, / That am already bruised, and shake / With terror sent from thee . . .?'(88.15–18; 57–60). This theme is basic to the question of Christian masculinity that has always concerned Milton. An aura of effeminacy attaches to these confessions of vulnerability, which are so foundational for Christian faith. Is the serious Christian man therefore deficient in manliness – is he, in contemporary parlance, *a bit gay*? Milton's concern, throughout his career, is to insist that the acceptance of one's dependence on God is part of true Christian masculinity. The weakness of God-dependence is balanced by the believer's participation, by means of rhetoric, in divine strength.

With the defeat of the royalist rising, the political atmosphere changed: there would be no return to a series of tortuous talks and deals, which Charles could scupper at will. Because his feet-dragging had caused new violence to break out, the king's image now changed. He had been seen as the rightful monarch, in thrall to evil advisers. If he backed down, and accepted constraints on his rule, all would be well. But now it seemed that he could not be trusted to return to a position of power. Cromwell now dubbed him 'that man of blood', a soundbite that sealed his fate. Finally the army took control; it effected a coup in December 1648, purging Parliament of the Presbyterians who had been plotting with the king. The new Parliament agreed to put the king on trial.

5

New Order

With the king in the dock, Milton returned to the political fray. In the last few years there had been little point in trying to influence public affairs: this new order was too disorderly. He had probably been taking a step back from politics and thinking through his theological position. Now things were, at last, moving forward again, and a bit of visionary prose might be in order. He wrote a new political tract, defending Parliament's tough line against the king, and attacking the Presbyterians' equivocation. In fact, this is what really prodded him into print: his renewed contempt for the Presbyterians. They had reacted to the king's trial by washing their hands. On 18 January 1649, English and Scots ministers had issued a joint document condemning the king's treatment, and likening it to the violence of the Jesuits. What irked Milton is that the same ministers had used the most extreme threatening rhetoric against the king and bishops: had they just been playing with words?

The Tenure of Kings and Magistrates is a forceful assertion of a nation's right to depose a tyrannical king. It draws on Aristotle and on the tradition of natural law that he inspired, and also on the post-Reformation growth of 'contractualist' political theory. This theory is based in a story, about free people choosing to create political authority, for the sake of security. Milton's assertion of the natural freedom of the citizen anticipates the revolutionary thought of a century later: 'No man who knows aught, can be so stupid to deny that all men naturally were born free.'[115]

---

115   Milton, *The Tenure of Kings and Magistrates*, CPW vol. 3, p. 201.

Kings and magistrates are the creatures of the people, who retain ultimate authority. Because rulers can abuse the power that is given to them, checks and balances are needed, and the most civilized nations have strong parliaments, through which the ruler is accountable to the people. Milton cites Aristotle's view that 'monarchy unaccountable is the worst sort of tyranny'.[116] Echoing the Roman thinker Sallust he observes that monarchy impedes the natural creativity of a people, its meritocratic potential.[117] And he also introduces biblical evidence, of God smiting kings who ignore his law. The New Testament echoes this in the Magnificat, Mary's foray into liberation theology. Christianity is intrinsically anti-tyrannical: 'Surely it is not for nothing that tyrants by a kind of natural instinct both hate and fear none more than the true Church and saints of God . . .'[118]

The Presbyterians ought to be familiar with all this for it is taught by all the reformers, says Milton. (As we saw in Chapter 1, Luther and Calvin were wary of advocating resistance but gradually saw that it might be necessary.) Now that the revolution is not under their control they question its legitimacy. '[N]ow that their censorious domineering is not suffered to be universal, truth and conscience to be freed, tithes and pluralities to be no more', they have the nerve to defend the king.[119] Have they forgotten that they 'hunted and pursued him round about the kingdom with sword and fire'?[120] In a nicely patronizing way, Milton takes this opportunity to dissuade the Presbyterians from their legalistic habits. He urges them not 'to affect rigour and superiority over men not under them, not to compel unforcible things, in religion especially, which if not voluntary, becomes a sin . . .'[121] *Please* try not to be such little fascists, he is saying. Soon he urges them 'not to be disturbers of the civil affairs, being in hands better able and more belonging to manage them; but to study harder, and to attend the office of good pastors . . .'[122]

---

116   Ibid., p. 204.
117   Quentin Skinner highlights Sallust's influence: Skinner, *Visions of Politics vol. 2, Renaissance Virtues,* Cambridge: Cambridge University Press 2002, p. 303.
118   Ibid., p. 217.
119   Ibid., p. 196.
120   Ibid., p. 231.
121   Ibid., p. 238.
122   Ibid., p. 240–1.

When he returns to the question of resisting tyrannical kings, Milton argues that God's deepest sympathies are not monarchist but republican. For when Israel decided to be a monarchy, it was a snub to God, who now had an earthly rival (1 Samuel 12). We can reasonably expect God to 'bless us, and be propitious to us who reject a king to make him [ie. God] only our leader and supreme governor in the conformity as near as may be of his own ancient government.'[123] He thus uses the Bible to challenge the assumption that regicide is an affront to divine order. Kings themselves are an affront to divine order. If God is making a new covenant with his favourite nation, then republicanism is likely to be part of it. We should not be afraid of doing something new: it means that we are setting a precedent that other nations may follow – a precedent that will make all future tyrants tremble on their thrones.

There is a hint of Lady Macbeth in this tract: a steely unflinching hardness that scorns coward doubts. This is what made Milton politically useful, from now on: his absolute refusal to be seduced by reactionary sentiment.

While the tract was at the printers, the momentous trial took place. Like all subsequent former rulers facing justice, Charles loftily dismissed the court's claim to authority. When asked for his plea, he replied, 'I would know by what power I am called hither', adding: 'I do stand more for the liberty of my people than any here that come to be my pretended Judges.' He refused 'to submit to a tyrannical or any other ways unlawful authority.' The court's verdict echoed the new theory of legitimacy: the king had broken his contract with the people. The death-sentence confirmed his martyr-complex: 'I am a martyr to the people', he said. He was executed on 30 January 1649.

Milton's justification for regicide was so admired among Cromwell's circle that he suddenly attained the reputation he had been seeking for the last eight years, and was invited to work for the new regime. In March 1649, he was appointed Secretary for Foreign Tongues to the Council of State, which largely involved translating and composing communications with foreign powers. But he was also commissioned to write new tracts.

---

123   Ibid.

A few months into the job, he was given an important commission. An immediate backlash against the new regime was gathering around a new bestseller. *Eikon Basilike* (The Image of the King) was a cult book in the fullest sense: it was the focus for the veneration of the late king, as a martyr. Thirty-five editions of this subversive book were produced in its first year. To the newly empowered radicals this was disturbing evidence of popular weakness, superstition, folly. A sentimental tract seemed to have conjured up a dangerously irrational movement. It reminds one of the reaction to a more recent royal death, that of Princess Diana. This ambiguous individual was ascribed a subversive sanctity in death. Many commentators, mostly conservatives, saw it as a sort of mob-madness, a decision for emotion over reason. This is how the progressives saw the mania surrounding the royalist book: it spoke of the craven servility built into the popular DNA. Milton's task was the exposure and exorcism of this.

Eikonoklastes invites the intelligent reader to disdain the tabloid-reading class, the 'blockish vulgar', for whom the celebrity-value of monarchy trumps all political considerations.[124] Later he lambasts 'an inconstant, irrational, and image-doting rabble.'[125] From the title on, Milton observes, this book is nakedly idolatrous; it exploits the fact that the people 'are prone ofttimes not to a religious only, but to a civil kind of idolatry in idolizing their kings.'[126] This anticipates the idea of monarchy as a 'political religion'.

Milton reiterates his case against Charles and his bishops, at very great length (this is a prose work that none could wish longer). It is of course more focused on Charles himself than any of the previous tracts; Milton is calmly determined to treat him as a flawed human being, responsible for the civil war. Charles' pose of dutifully defending the Church is attacked: 'Christian liberty purchased with the death of our Redeemer, and established by the sending of his free Spirit to inhabit in us, is not now to depend upon the doubtful consent of any earthly monarch, nor to

124   Milton, *Eikonoklastes*, CPW vol. 3, p. 339.
125   Ibid., p. 601.
126   Ibid., p. 343.

be again fettered with a presumptuous negative voice [ie. the monarch's power of veto].'[127] This is a good summary of his antipathy to the late king: the great task of our time, the reinvention of Christianity, must obviously not be subject to the will of this one unenlightened person. He shows how Charles presided over a Roman drift, how the very structure of the Church, and of the monarchy, made this inevitable.

Charles had posed as the defender of the Prayer Book: an opportunity for Milton to attack the very concept of liturgical fixity. The apostles decreed no such fixity; it is a clerical control-tool. 'God every morning rains down new expressions into our hearts', like he sent manna to the Jews: to fix liturgy is to horde manna, to let it 'breed worms and stink'.[128] Charles values the liturgy for its 'constancy', he sneers, 'as if it were constancy in the cuckoo always to be in the same liturgy'.[129] Milton's Christian anarchism is astonishing: does he really mean that there should be no official form of worship at all? Yes: he very firmly associates official religious forms with top-down religious structures, and it is hard to dispute the logic of this. Liturgical conservatism is a crucial tool of ecclesial conservatism: the orderly old ceremony must be kept up, and therefore so must the old institutional structures behind it. Milton's genius is to refuse to compromise with this traditionalist pathos; to refuse to be impressed. By contrast, the average so-called liberal Anglican claims to be pragmatic about tradition, but does not dare to break with its time-hallowed beauty. Milton knows and fears the aesthetic force of religious traditionalism.

Milton proceeds to attack the idea that the king, as 'God's anointed', is above the law. In the Bible, God issues laws that apply to all Israel, long before the emergence of monarchy. It is 'absurd to think that the anointment of God should be as it were a charm against law', for the law remains prior to any other political institution.[130] In all civilized states, a parliament embodies this superior authority, and, if there is a king, insists on his legal accountability. England's ancient traditions confirm 'that the king is under law, . . . that he stands as liable to receive justice as the

---

127   Ibid., p. 491–2.
128   Ibid., p. 505.
129   Ibid.
130   Ibid., p. 586.

meanest of his kingdom; . . . that laws both of God and man are made without exemption of any person whomsoever.'[131] As Quentin Skinner says, Milton 'is objecting to the very existence of the royal veto. To live under such a constitution is to live subject to the perpetual danger that the body politic will be moved to act by a will other than that of the nation as represented in parliament. But for a body to be subject to any will other than its own is for that body to be enslaved.'[132]

Charles' divinization of kingship is without biblical warrant: again Milton reminds us that biblical kings were often a threat to godly order. In effect, Milton is relocating 'divine right' from the monarch to the law of the land. The truly godly thing in politics is the universal authority of the law, from which no monarch or cleric is exempt. In other words, paradoxical as they sound, the authority of God is manifest in the authority of secular law – 'secular' because framed by a non-religious institution, Parliament.

The new republic had little popular support. Independency had little appeal beyond a small liberal elite. Cromwell had alienated the Levellers, with their democratic enthusiasm, and of course the Presbyterians were hostile. His military charisma continued to grow, with new victories in Ireland and Scotland, but while his popularity was confined to the army, and some liberals, he resembled a dictator. This is the paradox of the new regime: it presented itself as the defender of the liberty of the people, yet had minimal popular support, and had risen through curtailing the power of Parliament. This was a necessary temporary measure, said Cromwell, while Parliament was packed with royalist-sympathizing Presbyterians. The House of Lords was so clearly opposed to the king's trial that it had to be suspended. The defence of liberty requires seemingly authoritarian means, for the time being. It is common to see Cromwell as a sort of proto-fascist, using 'liberty' as an ideological self-justification. This is simplistic: his desire to bring a new liberal era was genuine. There is plenty of evidence to show that he really was motivated

---

131 Ibid., p. 592.
132 Quentin Skinner, *Liberty Before Liberalism*, Cambridge: Cambridge University Press 1998, p. 52–3.

by a vision of unprecedented toleration, however hard he found it to implement. His difficulty in realizing his tolerant ideal should not be overstated, and, despite his anti-Catholic rhetoric, '[t]he Roman Catholic minority found itself less persecuted in the Interregnum than under the monarchy.'[133]

The problem was that he had to rely heavily on the support of Presbyterians who did not share his liberal idealism. These conservatives convinced him of the necessity of a blasphemy law, and some notoriously strict moral reforms, including the prohibition of adultery. And they dissuaded him from reforming such things as mandatory church attendance, which was not lifted until three years into the Commonwealth. The new regime was therefore absurdly unbalanced – it was part Taliban, part liberal revolution. In his attempt to secure the triumph of the latter over the former, Cromwell found it necessary to be somewhat dictatorial.

Early in 1650, Milton was asked to refute another book – *Defensio Regia*, an attack on the new republic as a lawless regicidal dictatorship, and a call for European powers to take tough action against this rogue state. It was by a celebrated classical scholar called Salmasius. Milton's *Defence of the English People*, written in Latin as it addressed a European audience, was published in 1651. Salmasius had accused the new regime of bringing religious sectarianism. But it is not the role of the state to regulate religion, Milton replies. 'It is for this reason that war has followed war throughout our Christian world for so many years: namely, that magistrates and church are confused as to their jurisdictions.'[134] However, the state does have a role in suppressing religion that seeks political power. 'On this account particularly we cannot bear popery, for we know that it is less a religion than a priestly despotism under the cloak of religion, arrayed in the spoils of temporal power which it has violently appropriated in defiance of the clear teaching of Christ.'[135] Lasting peace can only come through the separation of church and state. This is the founding principle of liberalism. All forms of religion should

133   MacCulloch 2003, p. 527.
134   Milton, *A Defence of the People of England*, trans. by Donald C. Mackenzie, CPW vol. 4, p. 317.
135   Ibid., p. 321–2.

be tolerated as long as they acknowledge the authority of the state. It is a cliché of Milton criticism to point out that this famous advocate of toleration had an Achilles heel: he could not tolerate Catholicism. Such critics enjoy feeling superior to Milton, being free of his Romophobic prejudice. But this misses the point that Catholicism was politically dangerous, as it rejected the authority of the liberal state. It should be treated as a political rather than a religious movement. There is an obvious analogy with Islam today: we should be wary of tolerating Islamic extremism on political grounds, because it rejects the authority of the liberal state. Far from being illiberal, Milton's anti-Catholicism anticipated the contemporary awareness, currently returning through necessity, that liberalism must be robust to survive.

Salmasius had argued that Christian tradition is pro-monarchy. Actually, replies Milton, the Gospel is 'God's proclamation of our freedom . . . I do not speak of inward freedom only and omit political freedom . . . Christ put our political freedom on a firm foundation. In our place he assumed the form of a slave, but never failed to preserve the heart of a liberator.'[136] He sowed the seeds of liberty by teaching his disciples a new concept of authority (in Matthew 20:25). '"Ye know", he said, "that the princes of the Gentiles exercise dominion over them, and they that are great exercise authority upon them. But it shall not be so among you: but whosoever will be great among you, let him be your minister, and whosoever will be chief among you, let him be your servant." '[137] This is an important text for Milton. Christianity deconstructs political absolutism, or what might be called the *führer*-principle: it sees this form of politics as essentially pagan. Christians have to create a new sort of political authority, based on service. Some will object that Jesus was talking about religion rather than politics, but it is not clear-cut. Christian politicians can hardly ignore Christ's teaching, on the grounds that religion and politics are separate spheres. In a sense the 'separation of church and state' is paradoxical. It is only possible if the state is Christian, if it sees itself as a

---

136   Ibid., p. 374–5.
137   Ibid., p. 378.

sort of secular church. This is what Milton envisages: a state that rejects pagan absolutism in favour of truly Christian liberalism.

Towards the end of the book, Milton expresses, with new vehemence, his hatred of the infantilization that monarchy effects. It makes people weak, dependent:

> If you long for wealth, freedom, peace and power, would it not be much better . . . to strive resolutely for those ends through your own virtue, industry, prudence and courage than to hope for them in vain under a king's control? Surely those who suppose that these ends cannot be attained without a king and master must think of them-selves as unspeakably abject and ignoble, . . . spiritless and weak, bereft of intelligence and prudence, destined for slavery in body and soul.[138]

The rhetoric is almost Nietzschean – but of course he absolutely differs from Nietzsche in seeing Christianity as the antidote to servility. And is there not an American ring to this passage? Men should make their own way in the world, stand up for themselves, realize their full potential in the land of the free. 'When the Founding Fathers of the American republic spoke of "life, liberty and the pursuit of happiness", we think at least of the last as a post-enlightenment demand. But it was a demand which Milton would have understood.'[139]

The elephant in the room of the new regime was the reform of the Church. This is what the whole war had been about: the need to remove episcopacy. And Cromwell had seized power in order to prevent the Pres-byterians from becoming the new religious establishment. And of course this is why Milton supported him: he promised to move away from the concept of an official national Church of any description. Full-scale toleration meant that no religious orthodoxy would be imposed, that people would be free to worship however they wanted (as long as it did not threaten the security of the realm, as Catholicism did). So why, after a couple of years, was the old structure still pretty much in place? This is

---

138   Ibid., p. 532.
139   Christopher Hill, *Milton and the English Revolution*, p. 458.

what Milton must have been privately asking, with mounting alarm. A form of establishment lingered on, despite the removal of bishops, and the banning of the Prayer Book, and the killing of the king. It was now apparent that the structural essence of the old Church lay not in any of those things but in the system of tithes: the tax payable to the local parish church. The new regime had tried to sit on the fence: in 1649, it decreed that tithe-payment was voluntary rather than compulsory, but the following year it seemed to contradict this, passing an act allowing licensed ministers to receive tithes. It also passed a blasphemy act in this year: hardly a sign of a new era of toleration. But maybe these were emergency measures that Parliament would soon get round to repealing. Once its authority was secure, it could start dismantling the tithe system.

Milton was shaken out of this illusion at the beginning of 1652. Instead of being dismantled, the tithe system was given new official sanction. The republic was admitting that it needed it, for the foreseeable future. It needed it for two reasons: it was the basis of the rural economy, which was still largely feudal. The system did not just pay ministers' wages; it was the way in which the local squire taxed his dependants. The vested interests were too huge to contemplate offending. Also, the republic needed some sort of established Church in place if it was to have any hope of gathering public support. For the pulpit was a crucial tool of governmental communication. It needed the co-operation of the nine thousand parish ministers, who wanted the financial stability that tithes provided. So instead of dismantling the old religious structures, the republic wanted to use them. A new religious committee, led by John Owen, drew up a series of proposals for the regulation of the clergy. A post-episcopal state church was taking shape; a watered-down version of what the Presbyterians had wanted. Owen and his colleagues insisted that this would be a loose, open, tolerant state church, but surely any official church would gravitate towards the imposition of an orthodoxy? Owen and his colleagues were 'Independents' – this was the official religious ideology. But what did it mean? During the last ten years it had seemed to mean something like 'liberal Puritans' – those who wanted a freer, bishopless church, and resisted Calvinist fundamentalism. But once in power, hard choices had to be made about how to remake the national church. And it looked as if Independency would gravitate to Presbyterianism.

A new controversy arose. A scholar called Thomas Biddle had written a book that put Cromwell's warm words about toleration to the test. It argued against the doctrine of the Trinity. This doctrine has always been central to Christian 'orthodoxy', as asserted by the main churches, and its denial has been seen as theological poison. 'Arianism' was its main early expression: the denial that Jesus was fully God. The Reformation period saw a major outbreak of the heresy. The English Church was determined to give it no quarter. It was rigidly proscribed under Elizabeth, and when Milton was a boy of four, two men were executed for it (the last heretics to be burned in England). Anti-Trinitarianism was also known as Socinianism, after the Italian humanist Fausto Sozzini, who emigrated to Poland in the late sixteenth century, and established an anti-Trinitarian church. Poland was at this point a model of toleration – indeed only now, in the 1650s, was it cracking down on the heresy, having fallen under Counter-Reformation influence.

For hard-core liberal Protestants, the toleration of Socinianism was an important sign that Protestantism rejected the exclusionary logics of both Catholicism and Calvinism. Milton, in his official role of licenser, therefore approved the publication of Biddle's *Twofold Catechism* in February 1652. Such debates should be allowed. But most of the new regime was less sure. Cromwell's chief religious adviser, John Owen, thought the work should be suppressed, as it would endanger the Trinitarian faith of its readers. Ironically, he was probably right, in relation to its official licenser. It was probably Milton's engagement in this debate that led him towards his mature Arian position.

Milton realized that Biddle's book was an important test-case. His main concern was still tithes, but that was such a huge unwieldy problem (a bit like reforming British education today), that he cannot have expected instant results. But the toleration of Protestant 'heretics' was another matter: the government could instantly signal its commitment to freedom.

Milton began a campaign of reminding Cromwell, in general terms, where his true duties lay. Was the suppression of 'heresy' compatible with the toleration that Cromwell had promised? He put the rhetorical question to his leader and employer in sonnet form. It adapts the theme of his sonnet to Fairfax: the new task, after military victory, is the creation of a stable liberal state. The final couplet is a semi-veiled reference to the tithing issue:

> Help us to save free conscience from the paw
> Of hireling wolves whose gospel is their maw.

Is any minister who receives payment a 'hireling', motivated by greed? Is a state church necessarily inimical to religious liberty? Yes and yes, Milton implies. Cromwell had to be reminded of the radicalism he had espoused in opposition.

He also wrote a sonnet to Henry Vane, a politician in whom he had fuller confidence. Indeed Vane was heroized by various radical intellectuals: 'If there was a single hero of their lifetime for Ludlow, for Sidney, for Milton, it was Vane', writes Blair Worden. 'Over the course of the Long Parliament there was no more influential a member. He worked indefatigably for the war effort and outmanoeuvred those who sought accommodation with the king. Under the Commonwealth he carried out, with great energy and skill, the naval reforms that made Blake's triumphs possible.'[140] But what really appealed to Milton was his advocacy of religious liberty. He had come out clearly in defence of Biddle, and had recently written a treatise on the general question of religious freedom.

Vane had more authority than most to speak on the issue. Before the civil war, he had briefly been governor of Massachusetts, aged just twenty-three. He had tried to establish a high degree of toleration, but came up against Presbyterian orthodoxy, and was forced home. The story is worth a brief digression, as it shows that America's early religious history was marked by the very same issue that exercised Milton. The Massachusetts colony was founded in 1630 by a group of Puritans from East Anglia, led by John Winthrop (famous for predicting it would be 'a

---

140   Blair Worden, *Roundhead Reputations: The English Civil Wars and the Passions of Posterity*, Penguin 2001, p. 197.

city on a hill').[141] They were not quite separatists (unlike the Pilgrims who arrived on the Mayflower eight years earlier): they were officially loyal to the Church of England, though of course they demanded its reform. Laud tried to hold them to this official allegiance, but he was thousands of miles away and could be ignored. In effect, they founded a new province of Anglicanism, free from episcopal interference, and all the Rome-tainted liturgical rules. Instead of being a persecuted movement, these Puritans were suddenly founding a mini-state, in hostile conditions. They considered political and religious authority to be indistinguishable: the rules that defined church membership also defined citizenship; drunkards and adulterers were whipped, or worse. Some were banished, one man had his ears cut off for criticizing a minister (the punishment sometimes used by Laud). Incidentally there was a lively debate as to whether women should be veiled in public. It was a confessional community; a far tighter form of 'establishment' than existed anywhere in England. But it was unclear whether this rigour was a temporary necessity, or whether it would continue. Some urged the relaxation of such laws – and among the liberal voices was the idealistic young nobleman who arrived from England in 1635, Henry Vane. He was a popular figure, and the following year was elected governor. But a religious dispute broke out, and he found himself on the wrong side. A faction began to accuse the church authorities of legalism, of putting 'works' before grace. Vane, and one or two ministers, agreed that the matter should be looked into. But conservative Puritanism was roused: the dissenting faction, led by a woman called Anne Hutchinson, was accused of antinomianism, and sympathy with the anarchist Family of Love sect. In this political context, it seemed that a liberal critique of Puritanism was deeply threatening. And in a sense it was impossible, for there was no secular state to appeal to: the authority of the clergy was, in effect, the basis of politics. Inevitably perhaps, Hutchinson and her allies were accused of claiming superior spiritual authority to the ministers and politicians. And perhaps their dissent could only be expressed in such terms. Vane wanted to accommodate the dissenters,

---

141   See Francis J. Bremer, *John Winthrop: America's Forgotten Founding Father,* Oxford University Press 2003.

which would have entailed the creation of a new sort of secular space. But the tide was against him, so he returned to England in 1637. Hutchinson and her allies were banished, and the association between citizenship and allegiance to Puritan orthodoxy was tightened. Massachusetts decided that criticism of the religious authorities was intolerable. When the civil war broke out, Vane was an enthusiastic Independent: he knew from experience that the logic of Presbyterianism was anti-liberty. During the 1640s, he was one of the most outspoken Independent MPs, a champion of Milton's cause. And this is how Milton's sonnet celebrates him, as a classical republican hero, a senator. As well as being a great statesman, he is a pioneer of a new sort of political wisdom:

> . . . to know
> Both spiritual power and civil, what each means,
> What severs each, thou hast learned, which few have done.
> The bounds of either sword to thee we owe.
> Therefore on thy firm hand Religion leans
> In peace, and reckons thee her eldest son.

This is the true mark of the new, enlightened political élite: the resolute desire for a secular state, free of powerful religious institutions. And such men are more than just politicians: more than any priests, they defend the cause of true religion. We are so used to associating 'the separation of church and state' with America that it is rather strange to notice that Vane did not learn the principle in the new colony, but rather the opposite: he learned of its necessity, when he saw how the New England colonists tended in the direction of Calvinist tyranny. The separation of church and state was *England's* special vocation. How could the colonists show the way? Their idealism was tainted by the Swiss itch for theocracy.

Milton was at this time influenced by another American pioneer: Roger Williams, the founder of Rhode Island. He too was back in England now, campaigning for toleration (and teaching Milton Dutch). Rhode Island was the counterpoint to Massachusetts: Winthrop and Williams are the yin and yang of the America's soul. He founded an explicitly tolerant community in the late 1630s: it was to Rhode Island that Hutchinson and her fellow dissenters came. He was one of the very first people to put the principle of the separation of church and state into practice (although Rhode Island was more like a small town than a state). To uphold this principle was the state's duty: instead of pushing a unifying religious idea, it should protect the liberty of the various groups to worship as they chose. In his book of 1644, the oddly named *Bloudy Tenent, of Persecution, for cause of Conscience*, he had insisted that the supreme role of the state was to ensure 'that no persons, *Papists, Jewes, Turkes*, or *Indians* be disturbed at their worship, (a thing which the very *Indians* abhor to practice towards any)'.[142] It sounds like Thomas More's *Utopia*, in which perfect toleration exists among the imagined natives. Through talking to Williams in the early 1650s, Milton became more fully convinced that the separation of church and state was a sacred principle. Yet on the other hand, he did not believe that Williams' extreme liberalism could be brought home to England. He agreed with the Commonwealth's official position, that popery and prelacy were intolerable. Modern scholars who chide Milton for being incompletely liberal should accept that, when a nation is still in the process of purging itself of an authoritarian ideology, it can hardly offer that ideology toleration.

The real question was whether Cromwell's regime could protect religious liberty from the ever-present Presbyterian threat, and insist that all forms of Protestantism were valid. Parliament officially affirmed toleration for all Christians as long as 'they abuse not this liberty to the civil injury of others and to the actual disturbance of the public peace on their parts: provided this liberty be not extended to Popery or Prelacy, nor to such as, under the profession of Christ, hold forth and practice licentiousness.' Cromwell himself seemed determined to stand by this pledge. When a faction in Parliament sought to re-impose religious uniformity, he was furious: 'What greater hypocrisy than for those who were oppressed by the Bishops to become the greatest oppressors

---

142   Roger Williams, *The Bloudy Principle*, quoted in Thomas N. Corns, 'Milton, Roger Williams and the Limits of Toleration', in Achinstein and Sauer ed., *Milton and Toleration*, Oxford: Oxford University Press 2007, p. 77–8.

themselves so soon as this yoke was removed?'[143] The problem was that the instability of Parliament made religious policy unpredictable. In the summer of 1653, Cromwell replaced his failing Parliament with an assembly of religious nominees, modeled on the Jewish Sanhedrin. It was known as the Barebones Parliament, after one of its members, an eccentric preacher called Praise-God Barebones. But this only lasted six months. Cromwell was beginning to think that benign dictatorship was the only way to restore order. At this point some radicals, such as Vane, lost faith in him, insisting that the Commonwealth needed parliamentary legitimacy. This is the historiographical consensus, more or less: Cromwell turned tyrant, in his desperation to keep the revolution afloat. But Milton knew that there was no alternative but trusting Cromwell. He was assuming exceptional powers for the sake of establishing a new era of liberty, was he not? He was risking his reputation in order to make it work. Cromwell's sincerity cannot really be doubted. He told the odd new parliament, which looked like a holy quango, that 'if the poorest Christian, the most mistaken Christian shall desire to live peaceably and quietly under you – I say, if any desire but to lead a life of godliness and honesty, let him be protected.'[144] This was backed up by a new constitution, *The Instrument of Government*, which promised toleration for all 'such as profess faith in God by Jesus Christ.'

So Milton had grounds for hoping that, despite the collapse of the parliamentary system, the Commonwealth would keep pursuing liberty. And he could guide it, through his official work. There was another book to refute. It was called *The Cry of the Royal Blood to Heaven against the English Parricides*. As the tile hints, it was not a balanced assessment of the republic. It was by an English priest, still resident in the country, who obviously did not put his name to it. It was a response to Milton's recent *Defence of the English People*, full of vitriolic personal attacks on the official propagandist of the republic.

Milton's response, which appeared in 1654, is full of controlled aggression. As in *The Reason of Church Government* eleven years earlier, Milton

---

143   Quoted in Fraser 1973, p. 289.
144   Ibid., p. 433.

responds with an extensive and gently boastful autobiographical sketch. His antagonist had dismissed him as a pathetic little man, a wimp. So Milton replies that he is perfectly average, physically, and that he is kept in good shape. He had not been accused of dodging military service, but he addresses the issue anyway. He chose not to fight in the war because he felt he could be of more service as a writer. By lauding liberty's defenders he has played a crucial role in the struggle, he immodestly asserts, and by the way the Queen of Sweden is among his fans. His antagonist had clumsily jeered at his blindness, implying that it was a divine judgement on an immoral life. A perfect opportunity for Milton to speak of his carefully virtuous life, his selfless determination to serve his country. It is this that caused his blindness, for he was warned by doctors to stop working so hard, lest he lose his sight, but ignored them. Should he rise above the slurs aimed at him, he wonders? No, his readers must know 'that I am incapable of ever disgracing honorable speech by dishonorable conduct, or free utterances by slavish deeds, and that my life, by the grace of God, has ever been far removed' from all vice and crime.'[145] This echoes the claim in *An Apology for Smectymnuus* that a true writer 'ought himself to be a true poem'. Writing must be backed up by one's life: if one wants to speak of serious things, relating to religion and morality, one has to put one's life where one's mouth is. This principle horrifies contemporary creative writers.

He tells readers that he joined the anti-episcopal cause because it seemed 'a step towards the liberation of all human life from slavery – provided that the discipline arising from religion should overflow into the morals and institutions of the state.'[146] Liberty is in itself not enough – it lapses into license, and chaos. It is only a good idea to abolish ecclesiastical power if there is a strong Christian culture that will order people 'from within'. He also answers the charge that his political and religious vision is basically Anabaptist: 'equality in the state is not Anabaptist doctrine; it is democracy, a much more ancient thing. If established principally in the church, it is the apostolic discipline.'[147]

---

145 Milton, *A Second Defence of the English People*, trans. by Helen North, CPW vol. IV, p. 611.
146 Ibid., p. 622.
147 Ibid., p. 633.

The latter part of the book is concerned with defending England's new leaders, particularly Cromwell. His military greatness during the war was accompanied by great self-knowledge: 'whatever enemy lay within – vain hopes, fears, desires – he had either previously destroyed within himself or had long since reduced to subjection.'[148] Cromwell embodies the crucial point made above: that liberty must be founded on Christian discipline, on a moral revolution. He also illustrates the point made in the first *Defence*, that the Christian concept of political authority is based in humble service, rather than in the ruler's semi-divine status. Milton walks the tight-rope of telling Cromwell that he is greater than any king, due to his rejection of the monarchical style. To rule for the good of all, and 'to flee from the pomp of wealth and power, these are arduous tasks compared to which war is a mere game. These trials will buffet you [ie. Cromwell] and shake you; they require a man supported by divine help, advised and instructed by all-but-divine inspiration.'[149] Instead of ruling by divine right, he must rule by divine inspiration.

Milton now reminds him of the guiding principle he must uphold:

> I would have you leave the church to the church and shrewdly relieve yourself and the government of half your burden (one that is at the same time completely alien to you), and not permit two powers, utterly diverse, the civil and the ecclesiastical, to make harlots of each other and while appearing to strengthen, by their mingled and spurious riches, actually to undermine and at length destroy each other. I would have you remove all power from the church (but power will never be absent so long as money, the poison of the church, the quinsy of truth, extorted by force even from those who are unwilling, remains the price of preaching of the Gospel).[150]

What he means by leaving the church to the church is resisting the urge to create a state church. The problem was that England's religious life naturally gravitated in this direction, thanks to the tithe system. So

---

148   Ibid., p. 667.
149   Ibid., p. 674.
150   Ibid., p. 678.

Cromwell's task is actually to confront this tendency, to dismantle the centripetal force of tithes. Instead of leaving religion alone, he must go out of his way to de-centralise it, to stop a new official version from arising. And here, precisely, is the great tragedy of Milton's political life: this was unrealistic. The new regime could not afford to unsettle the economic order in this way, to anger the tax-gathering squires, who were already vaguely hostile to the republic.

The state should limit its role, he goes on; it should beware of making too many laws: it should not ban things just because they are open to abuse: 'for laws are made only to curb wickedness, but nothing can so effectively mould and create virtue as liberty.'[151] This brings him on to the fundamentalists, 'who do not believe themselves free unless they deny freedom to others, and who do nothing with greater enthusiasm or vigour than cast into chains, not just the bodies, but also the consciences of their brothers, and impose on the state and the church the worst of all tyrannies, that of their own base customs or opinions'.[152] And he continues, with great relevance to the contemporary debate about faith communities' demand for exemption from the secular law:

> May you always take the side of those who think that not just their own party or faction, but all citizens equally have an equal right to freedom in the state. If there be any man for whom such liberty, which can be maintained by the magistrates, does not suffice, he is, I judge, more in love with self-seeking and mob-rule than with genuine liberty, for a people torn by so many factions . . . does not itself permit that condition in public affairs which is ideal and perfect.[153]

We must assert the full authority of universal secular law, and be wary of those who resist it. But where Milton differs from the modern secularist is in insisting that liberty must be rooted in personal piety. He concludes with a sermon directed at his countrymen. Unless liberty 'has

151   Ibid.
152   Ibid., p. 678–9.
153   Ibid., p. 679–80.

was taken from him; he was now a disabled single parent of three young daughters.

In September 1654, Cromwell launched a new parliament, but it was little more than an appendage to his Council of State. The following year there was an increased fear of royalist risings, and Cromwell reacted by tightening his grip on the nation, by means of 'Major Generals', powerful local deputies. There were effectively authorized to keep the peace by whatever means they deemed necessary. Their main task was to prevent gatherings of royalists (horse-races and other sporting events were banned, as they often provided cover for political rallies). But some, especially those with Presbyterian sympathies, were keen to create a new religious uniformity. That meant cracking down on the sectarian Protestants who opposed the official Church. Many of these sects had incubated in Cromwell's army, most notably the Levellers. Groups such as the Familists proclaimed that all worldly bonds could be loosened, as the Kingdom of God was on the horizon, and other groups such as the Fifth Monarchy Men spoke of an imminent divine revolution. The Diggers had set up their communes. In many sects there was a shockingly high presence of women in positions of authority (a rare mark of freedom that Milton frowned on). Some sects preached universal salvation, and a sort of utopian humanism known as the Everlasting Gospel. The Seekers were radical Independents, who opposed all forms of religious organization: they overlapped with the Ranters, anarchists whose subversive religiosity (or anti-religiosity) entailed swearing, cursing, alcohol and sexual license. They disrupted Winstanley's Digger community with free-love. The young John Bunyan was briefly tempted to join. These sects had been a feature of national life since the civil war, and showed no sign of abating in the republic. How far should they be tolerated? The republic was intent on tolerating all sincere Protestants, but did this extend to Ranters, who seemed to want to offend mainstream Christians? The 1650 Blasphemy Act was designed to curb these religious punks. But their influence had spread to a new movement that was less easy to dismiss.

The movement began with George Fox, an itinerant preacher who heckled priests, and got into scraps with their congregations. He sometimes displayed his prophetic status by shaking with humble fervour at the thought of divine authority: hence his followers' nickname, Quakers. He seems to have attracted ex-Levellers, those who still wanted the world turned upside down. His teaching was certainly politically subversive: he attacked the tithe system, and rejected all conventions of social hierarchy, especially the tradition of tipping one's hat when greeting a social superior. He was aggressively informal; he addressed everyone as 'thou', rather like calling everyone 'mate'. His mobility was crucial to the new creed: he did not want to create stable settled congregations but a gaseous movement. Its aim was to challenge religious institutionalism. The true church was completely anti-authoritarian. Fox called churches 'steeple-houses' to show that they had nothing to do with the true spiritual church. His theology was minimalist: he saw doctrinal orthodoxy and the Puritan appeal to the Bible as tools of institutional authoritarianism. The Word of God was free from the written text, and from all religious forms. And he also reacted against the Puritan emphasis on sin: once the believer had rejected the sinful world, said Fox, he was united with Christ. In effect he announced that the kingdom of God had arrived, at least for the pure elect. He therefore rejected the necessity of war, and, to a large extent, secular law. In this new age the Gospel alone was authoritative. In particular, he denounced the swearing of oaths, which was still a basic tool of military and political order. Unlike his Puritan enemies, he was a fundamentalist about toleration.

Cromwell, to the bafflement of most of his colleagues, admired Fox. He met him a few times, and reassured him that his movement was a valid part of the new religious landscape. The Presbyterians, on the other hand, saw the Quakers as the principal threat to their gradual take-over of the established Church. They influenced a new hard-line approach. In 1655, Parliament issued a proclamation against 'divers men lately risen up under the names of Quakers, Ranters, and others, who do daily both reproach and disturb the assemblies and congregations of Christians in their public and private meetings and interrupt the preachers in dispensing the word and others in their worship contrary to just liberty and to the disturbance of the public peace.'

Milton had mixed feelings about these radicals. He was deeply sympathetic to their anti-institutionalism, their opposition to tithes, yet he feared that they were giving his cause a bad name, by linking it to an irrational, emotive religiosity. Religious radicalism ought to be calm, intelligent, not a raucous riot, with embarrassing displays of inspiration. Religious radicalism was meant to be developing an establishment aura, and this counter-cultural circus was not helping. In a properly Protestant republic, this sort of sectarianism ought not to be happening, for the Christian's loyalty ought to be to the state rather than to a 'pure' subculture within it. He feared, with justification, that the rise of the Quakers would strengthen the hand of the Presbyterians – and the royalists. It would persuade the ruling class that sectarianism was a threat to order, that an official national church was necessary.

Milton agreed with Cromwell that a national Protestant ideology had to be cultivated – a new version of Elizabeth's strutting of the world stage. The nation had to defend European Protestantism, ever-threatened by Catholic violence, and also it had to challenge Spain's hold on the new world. This global perspective was central to the Commonwealth ideology. Domestic civil liberties had to be balanced by another consideration: the need to make the world safe for Protestantism. Cromwell was increasingly determined to fight Spain for control of America, and the West Indies was the prime theatre of the struggle. In 1655, Milton, in his official capacity, helped to draft the *Manifesto* justifying the declaration of war against Spain. It cited the Catholic power's maltreatment of the natives: it was right to avenge their blood 'since God has made of one blood all nations of men for to dwell on all the face of the earth . . . All great and extraordinary wrongs done to particular persons ought to be considered as in a manner done to all the rest of the human race.'[156] This high rhetoric was somewhat ironic, seeing as Cromwell proposed to colonise Jamaica using enslaved Irishmen. This is the origin of the liberal intervention dilemma, which has been writ large in our time: does the end (the most liberal powers dominating the world) justify the means (their use of methods associated with their less liberal enemies)? Milton was basically loyal to Cromwell's proto-Blairite idealism, but as we shall see his qualms about imperialism emerged in his epics.

---

156   Quoted in Christopher Hill, *Puritanism and Revolution*, London: Pimlico (1958), 2001, p. 135.

In the spring of 1655, the case for liberal interventionism was strengthened, when a distant massacre reminded all Protestants of the common enemy. The Waldensians of the Piedmont region in the southern Alps were the oldest surviving culture in Europe that could be described as protestant. Foxe had praised them. Their defiance of Rome had begun in the twelfth century, but they were too small and isolated to pose much of a threat, and the Church let them be for centuries. But the upheavals of the Reformation made them vulnerable, and they began to be harassed by the local power, Savoy. In April 1655, Duke Carlo Emanuale II of Savoy allowed a massacre to take place. It would nowadays be described as ethnic cleansing, perhaps genocide, and Protestant Europe was duly horrified. Cromwell led the international outcry (Milton was involved in composing the diplomatic documents), and it was a major domestic news story that led to the raising of an emergency relief fund – the original emergency aid appeal. Like the Tibetans today, the Waldensians were seen as an ancient peace-loving mountain people. Also, of course, they represented a particularly pure form of Protestantism, free of the institutional rigidity of most of the Reformation. This is what Milton highlighted in his sonnet that begins, 'Avenge, O Lord, thy slaughtered saints . . .'. They 'kept thy truth so pure of old / When all our fathers worshiped stocks and stones . . .' Milton is generally adamant that true Protestantism has English roots, so this is high praise. The violence of the massacre is sketched in the simple image of their bones 'scattered on the Alpine mountains cold'. There is something very modern about this focus on the randomness, the disorder, the horror. And there is also a very raw, primal feel to the lament: as Elizabeth Sauer observes, '[t]he octave's end rhymes reinforce the elegiac nature of the verses: "bones", "cold", "old", "stones", "groans", "fold", "rolled", "moans". Sonically, then, the poem is dominated by the "o" sound which both begets and sustains its avalanche.'[157] Some secularist critics will say that Milton hides from the full horror, through believing that divine justice makes everything all right in the end. Actually this sonnet ought to be proof against such a clichéd dismissal of a religious viewpoint. There is no sense that the horror is mitigated

---

157   Elizabeth Sauer, 'Toleration and Nationhood in the 1650s', in Achinstein and Sauer 2007, p. 214.

because the victims have gone to heaven. Instead, their blood cries out. Their murder necessitates a future act of God, in this world (the downfall of the papacy, as prelude to the Second Coming). In imitation of the Psalms, Milton has to shout at God, to hector him into action. Yes, the poem shows trust in divine providence, but trust cannot be dismissed as facile when it's expressed in the form of orders: 'Avenge . . . Forget not . . . record . . . sow'. Is Milton struggling to believe in God's justice? In a sense: to have faith in God is intrinsically agonistic; it entails a violent speech-act – ordering God around, predicting divine violence. It might be described as wishful thinking, of a sort, but it can hardly be called comfy, complacent or consoling.

If Milton cared so much about overseas victims of state violence, critics have asked, why did he not complain about the plight of the Irish? They were being dispossessed, even enslaved, to smooth the 'plantation' of Protestants. This sonnet is tacitly justifying that process, by demonizing Catholicism as intrinsically tyrannical. By studying it 'in the context of English cultural politics of the day, we discover how "the blood of the martyrs becomes the seed of colonialism" ', says one recent critic.[158] It should be admitted that Milton's reaction to international suffering is not exactly neutral. He was guilty of seeing Protestants as more fully human than Catholics, and of believing that the end justified the means in Ireland: England's 'back door' had to be secured against Catholic invasion, by whatever force necessary. The situation is closely analogous to contemporary Israel: the chosen people cannot let itself be snuffed out.

If the fate of the Waldensians helped to unite England's Protestants, it was not for very long. The Presbyterians were becoming increasingly nervous about the rise of the Quakers. Like a modern cult the movement was held together by Fox's charisma. But even a charismatic figure will struggle to keep a nation-wide movement together. In 1656, a splinter group emerged under James Nayler. He was egged into sub-cult leadership by an astonishingly feisty young woman called Martha Simmonds, whose real vocation was avant-garde theatre, in the form of prophetic signs, sacramental 'happenings'.

---

158   Ibid., p. 223.

On 24 October 1656, this splinter-group staged a piece of religious theatre that demonstrated the limits of toleration. They staged Jesus' entry into Jerusalem, in Bristol. Nayler (playing Jesus) was brought to London, and tried by a special committee of MPs and Major Generals. The Presbyterians in Parliament were keen to make an example of him. The religious right wanted blood. Cromwell was not feeling strong enough to resist them; he took a back seat, and drifted into the role of Pontius Pilate. The key question at the trial was whether Nayler was claiming to be the Second Coming. He denied it, but repeated the Quaker maxim that he had 'that of God' in him, that the true believer took on the identity of Christ. In the circumstances this sounded suspicious. In the striking phrase of one accuser, this divine impersonation was 'the ungodding of God'. The committee convicted him of blasphemy, and many pressed for the death penalty. In an amazing irony they argued that the biblical penalty for blasphemy was death. The Jews had therefore been right to demand the death of Jesus – where they got it wrong was failing to see that Jesus really was the Messiah and not an impostor. In the end, they narrowly voted against the death penalty. Cromwell urged exile, but the favoured penalty was whipping, branding and the boring of the tongue with a hot iron. This occurred on 27 December 1656.

The entire episode would have confirmed Milton's sense that it is better to tolerate strange religious expressions, as far as it is politically possible, and that the desire to stamp on them is anti-Christian. As he had said over a decade ago, 'woe to us, while, thinking thus to defend the Gospel, we are found the persecutors.'[159] The real danger is not the potential blasphemy of Nayler, but the blasphemy of turning the Gospel into a theocratic ideology.

In fact his mind was elsewhere in October 1656: he got married again, to the twenty-eight year old Katherine Woodcock. The following October she bore him a baby girl. He had been granted another chance at marital happiness. If the Commonwealth managed to stabilize, he could look forward to a calm and contented retirement.

---

159 Milton, *Areopagitica,* p. 568.

6

In Retreat

In February 1658, after just fifteen months of being Mrs. Milton, Katherine died, and soon afterwards the baby died too. He seems to have loved her: the chief evidence is the sonnet he wrote following her death; it relates a dream in which he sees her again – or rather in which he sees her for the first time, or half-sees her, for her angelic purity veils her from him; it is a foretaste of heaven, of seeing 'face to face'. The climax is almost melodramatic: as she moved to embrace him, 'I waked, she fled, and day brought back my night'. As I suggested earlier, his blindness is tied up with a new spiritual and emotional frankness, an acceptance of vulnerability.

It is worth pausing here, at his last sonnet, to note the importance of the sonnets he had written since the beginning of the civil war. In a sense they are more influential on subsequent English poetry than his epics. What is new is that a grand style is applied to both personal and political concerns. There is aesthetic intensity, but it is not for the decoration of a fairy-world, nor is it locked into the affected rhetoric of the love sonnet: it is in the service of honest, urgent reflection. Shakespeare's sonnets are often psychologically intense as well as aesthetically rich, but they exude the falsity of a genre; the poet is playing a game, wearing a mask (this also applies to Donne). The miracle of Milton's sonnets is that the grand style feels natural, rooted in the political world; it feels like a special form of ordinary speech. He uses a lofty style, with serene classical imagery and prophetic imitation, not in order to pose but in order to speak *as himself.*

He is preparing the way for Wordsworth, Keats and Yeats. It is hardly an exaggeration to say that his sonnets invent the dominant voice of modern poetry, that might be summed up as grand sincerity. For Wain, 'the parallel is clearly with Yeats, another poet whose manner is often described as lofty and grand . . . but who turns out on inspection to be not in the least afraid of plain, familiar language.'[160]

This year brought another death, whose consequences were just as depressing. Oliver Cromwell, the Lord Protector, died, and was replaced by his unimpressive son Richard. A grand state funeral masked the Commonwealth's new precariousness.

Had Milton kept believing in Cromwell? Through gritted teeth, but yes, for there was no alternative. He simply had to be trusted, for the revolution depended on him. He had praised him to the skies in the *Second Defence* of 1654, but the praise is full of anxiety about whether the republic can really survive. He begs his fellow Englishmen to keep faith in the revolution, and its leader: 'If the republic should miscarry, so to speak, and as quickly vanish, surely no greater shame and disgrace could befall this country.'[161] Soon the effort of belief became even harder, with the emergence of the Major Generals, and England's new resemblance to a police state. It took the blindest faith to believe that lasting liberty would emerge from this authoritarianism, that an end was in sight that would justify the means. The Commonwealth had not put down strong enough roots to survive. As he had said in the *Second Defence*, liberty depended on a new religious spirit possessing the people at large. It seemed that it had not. What about his cherished principle of the separation of church and state? It had been badly botched: there had been a grim drift towards a semi-Presbyterian established Church. But the principle was still paid official lip-service: that was something. It was still possible for a public intellectual to call for this ideal's fuller realization.

Richard Cromwell failed to sustain the Protectorate, and the Rump Parliament reconvened. Milton tried to see this as a hopeful development. Maybe the republic would have a second wind, with Parliament

---

160   John Wain, 'Strength and Isolation: Pessimistic Notes of a Miltonolater', in Kermode 1960, p. 4.
161   Milton, *The Second Defence of the English People*, CPW vol. 4, p. 673.

restored to its proper sovereignty. Early in 1659, he began work on a pair of tracts addressed to Parliament. The first, *A Treatise of Civil Power in Ecclesiastical Causes*, argues that Christianity is corrupted by compulsion: if a state tries to enforce the Gospel, it falsifies it. Of course the Catholic ruler corrupts the Gospel in this way: what is more scandalous is the way in which 'the forcing protestant' imitates him; 'the more he professes to be a true protestant, the more he has to answer for his persecuting than a papist.'[162] It is a failure of trust in Christ, to think that the Gospel will wither away 'unless it be enacted and settled, as they call it, by the state, a statute or a state-religion.'[163] Those who advocate a unity of church and state are reverting to the Old Testament model: 'If church and state shall be made one flesh again as under the law, let it be withal considered, that God who then joined them hath now severed them'; to rejoin them after their New Testament separation would be 'presumptuous fornication.'[164]

The accompanying tract, *Considerations Touching the Likeliest Means to Remove Hirelings out of the Church*, is concerned with the cardinal error of mandatory public funding for the clergy. While the practice persists, 'I dare affirm that no model whatsoever of a commonwealth will prove successful or undisturbed.'[165] The rot began with Constantine, 'who out of his zeal thinking he could be never too liberally a nursing father of the church, might be not unfitly said to have ... choked it in the nursing.'[166] The theologians of this era made Christianity into a worldly religion, 'whereby thinking to gain all, they lost all: and instead of winning Jews and pagans to be Christians, by too much condescending they turned Christians into Jews and pagans.'[167] There is obviously no biblical warrant for the funding of clergy by the tithe system. The true church cannot be tied to a political territory in this way, for it consists 'of many particular churches complete in themselves; gathered ... by free

162 Milton, *A Treatise of Civil Power in Ecclesiastical Causes*, CPW vol. 7, p. 256.
163 Ibid., p. 259.
164 Ibid., p. 261.
165 Milton, *Considerations Touching the Likeliest Means to Remove Hirelings out of the Church*, CPW vol. 7, p. 275.
166 Ibid., p. 279.
167 Ibid., p. 294.

consent.'[168] A tithe system necessarily entails an official institution impos-
ing uniformity throughout the nation, and so the loss of 'Christian lib-
erty'. Instead of expecting state funding, ministers should imitate the
Waldensian preachers, 'the ancient stock of our reformation' – they
always practiced trades, especially medicine.[169] State funding puts the
church at the mercy of politicians: they 'will pay none but such whom by
their committees of examination, they find conformable to their interest
and opinions.'[170] If the state controls religion, 'how can any Christian
object it to a Turk, that his religion stands by force only; and not justly
fear from him this reply, yours by both force and money in the judgement
of your own preachers? This is that which makes atheists in the land . . .:
not the want of maintenance or preachers, as they allege, but the many
hirelings and cheaters that have the gospel in their hands.'[171] Here Milton
anticipates the coming intellectual revolution, the secular Enlightenment:
an inauthentic church, imposed from above rather than rooted in popu-
lar piety, is bound to result in the rise of atheism.

By the autumn the Rump Parliament was collapsing: the army briefly
took over, then withdrew. Anarchy loomed. A quiet consensus was form-
ing: only the restoration of the monarchy could restore order. The
experiment had failed, and almost everyone knew it. In January 1660, a
deus ex machina arrived on the scene: General Monck, commander of
the army in Scotland. He recalled the Rump, forcing it to re-admit royal-
ist sympathizers. He organized a convention to decide the nation's future:
it was an open secret that the king would be restored. It was time for
Milton to move towards the fence, or simply kept quiet. Smoother types
like Dryden and Marvell began to dust down their royalism; to say that
peace and order were what mattered, and one had to be pragmatic.

Milton was one of the few people in England who believed that the
republican cause could be salvaged. Instead of burning his papers, and
fleeing to some rural retreat, he rushed a new polemic to the press. *The
Ready and Easy Way to Establish a Free Commonwealth* is a last-ditch

---

168   Ibid., p. 293.
169   Ibid., p. 306.
170   Ibid., p. 318.
171   Ibid., p. 319.

attempt to rally the nation in defense of republicanism, before it is too late. If we fail now, we will seem to the rest of Europe like 'that foolish builder mentioned by our Saviour, who began to build a tower, and was not able to finish it. Where is this goodly tower of a commonwealth, which the English boasted they would build to overthrow kings, and be a new Rome in the west?'[172]

A free republic is the Christian version of politics, he reiterates:

> ... wherein they who are the greatest, are perpetual servants and drudges to the public at their own cost and charges, neglect their own affairs, yet are not elevated above their brethren; live soberly in their families, walk the street as other men, may be spoken to freely, familiarly, friendly, without adoration. Whereas a king must be adored like a demigod, with a dissolute and haughty court about him, of vast expense and luxury, masks and revels, to the debauching of our prime gentry, both male and female.[173]

Under a monarchy, people who could have served the public will clamour to be court servants, 'grooms even of the close-stool.'[174] People who could be teachers or doctors will be fighting for the chance to wipe the king's bum. Look at the French court, 'where enticements and preferments daily draw away and pervert the Protestant nobility.'[175] The need for a monarch speaks of pathetic weakness: 'How unmanly must it needs be, to count such a one the breath of our nostrils, to hang all our felicity on him, all our safety, all our well-being, for which if we were aught else but sluggards or babies, we need depend on none but God and our own counsels, our own active virtue and industry!'[176] How can a Christian society tolerate this? Christ specifically forbade 'such gentilish imitation' in his followers: the new chosen people must reject pagan politics. Monarchy usurps the authority of Christ in the state, just as the papacy

---

172 *The Ready and Easy Way to Establish a Free Commonwealth*, CPW vol. 7, p. 422–3.
173 Ibid., p. 425.
174 Ibid.
175 Ibid., p. 426.
176 Ibid., p. 427.

usurps it in the Church. The implication, again, is that the reformed Christian state is a sort of church.

He sketches a political blueprint: there should be an elected grand council, in perpetual session. Senators should stay for life. Only by recreating the Roman republic can we find lasting stability. With 'temporal and spiritual lords removed', our liberty will be secure.[177] If monarchy returns, it will not be a new, restrained monarchy, as some are now arguing: instead, our future kings, 'never forgetting their former ejection, will be sure to fortify and arm themselves sufficiently for the future against all such attempts hereafter from the people.'[178] Things will be worse than before.

God wants us free to worship him as we see fit: 'the whole Protestant church allows no supreme judge or rule in matters of religion, but the Scriptures; and these to be interpreted by the Scriptures themselves, which necessarily infers liberty of conscience.'[179] Monarchs cannot tolerate this sort of freedom. Elizabeth was better than most monarchs, but she suppressed reformers. 'What liberty of conscience can we then expect from other [monarchs], . . . trained up and governed by popish and Spanish counsels . . .?'[180]

His conclusion is sombre. He has said his piece: even if he knew no one was listening he'd still feel compelled to say it anyway, to cry 'with the prophet, "O earth, earth, earth!", to tell the very soil itself, what her perverse inhabitants are deaf to.'[181] He seems to feel that this might be his last chance of public utterance, so he had better take it, come what may.

His rashness had limits. He did not publicize the full extent of his radicalism. Among his personal papers was a theological work that had been in progress for at least a decade. *De Doctrina Christiana* is a long exposition of his radical theology, full of scriptural reference. It was never published in his lifetime; the manuscript was only discovered in 1823 (when it caused a stir among his pious admirers). The fact that he wrote

---

177   Ibid., p. 445.
178   Ibid., p. 449.
179   Ibid., p. 456.
180   Ibid., p. 457.
181   Ibid., p. 462–3.

it in Latin suggests that he envisaged an eventual audience throughout Europe, that he wanted this work to affect the course of international Protestantism. It was probably first conceived in the late 1640s, when he wrote very little for publication, and was prodded by Presbyterianism into developing his religious thought; and he probably returned to it in the late 1650s, as he became gradually released from official duties. According to Christopher Hill, Milton saw it as 'the legacy of free England to the Protestant world, all that could be salvaged from the wreckage of God's cause in the chosen nation.'[182] Milton himself called it 'his dearest and best possession.'

Its preface resembles one of Paul's epistles: it is addressed to all churches, and all who profess faith in Christ; it ends by urging its readers 'to live in the spirit of our Lord and Saviour Jesus Christ.'[183] It's a significant bit of impersonation: Milton is trying to get back to the very early days of Christianity, before any form of institutional orthodoxy had emerged. What follows is a personal view, he explains: it originates in the conviction that 'God has revealed the way of eternal salvation only to the individual faith of each man, and demands of us that any man who wishes to be saved should work out his beliefs for himself. So I made up my mind to puzzle out a religious creed for myself by my own exertions . . .'[184] Some of his conclusions might be unconventional, but 'I implore all friends of truth not to start shouting that the church is being thrown into confusion by free discussion and inquiry.'[185]

He lays much emphasis on rejecting Calvin's determinism, preferring the Arminian position that we have free will. His thinking on this issue changed during the 1640s: he had previously been suspicious of Arminianism as crypto-Catholic, and implied his agreement with the Calvinists. But his falling out with the Presbyterians had led him to associate predestination with their general fundamentalism. Of course predestination makes God seem cruel, for planning the damnation of the damned, but Milton's real complaint is that it makes God seem illiberal. His belief in

182 Christopher Hill, *Milton and the English Revolution*, London: Faber 1977, p. 234.
183 Milton, *Christian Doctrine*, trans. by John Carey, CPW vol. 6, p. 124.
184 Ibid., p. 118.
185 Ibid., p. 121.

religious and cultural liberty led him to insist that God, the inventor of liberty, has made us free to decide for or against him. Our free will does not detract from divine omnipotence, for God knows in advance what we will freely do. In *Paradise Lost* he allows God to explain this for Himself.

He prefaces Chapter Five with a restatement of the principle of theological liberty:

> The Roman Church demands implicit obedience on all points of faith. If I professed myself a member of it, I should be so indoctrinated, or at any rate so besotted by habit, that I should yield to its authority . . . As it happens, however, I am one of those who recognize God's word alone as the rule of faith; so I shall state quite openly what seems to me much more clearly deducible from the text of scripture than the currently accepted doctrine. I do not see how anyone who calls himself a Protestant or a member of the Reformed Church . . . could be offended with me for this, especially as I am not trying to browbeat anyone, but am merely pointing out what I consider the more credible doctrine.[186]

Protestantism ought to reject the concept of orthodoxy, if orthodoxy means an official version of doctrine that the believer is dissuaded from questioning. The location of authority in scripture ought to make 'orthodoxy' redundant, for there will always be legitimate debates over its interpretation. The reason for underlining this again is that he is about to broach his dissent from the doctrine of the Trinity, to advocate the major heresy of Arianism. Mainstream Christianity defined itself against this heresy at the fourth-century Council of Nicaea, insisting that the Father, Son and Holy Spirit are all fully God. Milton insists that the Son and the Spirit are inferior to the Father, created by him. It is irrational to think that God is simultaneously one and three, and there are no scriptural grounds for it. Of course he does not actually question Jesus' divinity (a large amount of his poetry is based around asserting Jesus' divinity), just the Son's equality with the Father. Why does he think it so important

---

186   Ibid., p. 203.

to reject orthodox teaching? To call the Trinity irrational begs certain Dawkins-type questions. It seems that he is partly motivated by the desire to put his 'orthoclastic' principle into practice, to remind us that theological custom might be 'agedness of error'. He wants to break a taboo: centuries of convention decree that real Christianity is Trinitarian, but there are no obvious grounds for this assumption. Instead of revering tradition, and swallowing whatever priests tell us, let's open it to scrutiny – let's *think about it*. His rhetoric is confrontational: the Trinity is 'a bizarre and senseless idea'.[187] By questioning the judgement of the Council of Nicaea he is also questioning the entire Constantinian tradition (the Emperor Constantine convened the council). As we saw, he regards Constantine as the villainous architect of established religion. The Trinity is so steeped in assertions of ecclesial power that it is safer to reject it. If one accepts it, one might start warming to the whole tradition of an authoritative institution defending 'orthodoxy' from the dangerous heretics.

His Arianism also seems motivated by his belief in God's absolute authority. As we have often seen, this is the essence of Christian faith for him, and his republicanism intensifies it. He insists that true absolutism belongs here alone. His doctrinal amendment also allows him to foreground the theme of obedience. It is important to him that the Son models perfect obedience to the Father, and this, as he sees it, is obscured by the normal conception. Only a distinct person can really obey another.

His view of creation is also unorthodox: the conventional teaching that God created the world 'from nothing' is seen as irrational. He must have used part of himself. This leads to a fuller belief in the essential goodness of created matter. This rejection of dualism is taken even further in his belief about the afterlife. The soul dies with the body, and the two are resurrected together at the Last Day – a view known as 'mortalism'. Incidentally, mainstream theology has largely come round to mortalism in recent decades, and rejected the otherworldly dualism of the idea of the soul going to a disembodied heaven.[188]

---

187   Ibid., p. 212.
188   See for example Tom Wright, *Surprised by Hope*, London: SPCK 2007, *passim*.

Some other provocative heresies are offered: polygamy is acceptable, as it occurs in the Old Testament and is not forbidden in the New. Often as he appeals to scripture, Milton is no biblical fundamentalist: as we have seen he is more concerned than most Protestants to reject the legalism of the Old Testament, and even interprets away Jesus' seeming prohibition of divorce. He is more interested in using the Bible *negatively* – to counter traditional claims to Christian authority, than *positively*, to argue for new moral and doctrinal rules.

If the individual believer, with his Bible, is sovereign, does the church have any authority at all? No: not if the church is understood as a worldly institution. The true church is mystical; the 'invisible church' of all true believers. 'It need not be subject to spatial considerations: it includes people from many remote countries, and from all ages since the creation of the world.'[189] The visible church is described in very general terms: it is all those 'who openly worship God the Father in Christ either individually or in conjunction with others.' *Individually*? 'Although it is the duty of every believer to join himself, if possible, to a correctly instituted church . . ., those who are not able to do so conveniently, or with a good conscience, are not therefore excluded from or destitute of the blessing which was bestowed on the churches.'[190] There cannot be many sketches of ecclesiology that are so quick to accommodate awkward individualists! In effect, he is using 'church' to mean 'authentic Christian culture'. And of course it has no central authority structure, no leader. Are coherent organizations not needed to administer the sacraments? No. The sacraments have been idolized by the Catholic Church, in order to cement its power, and Protestantism is still somewhat in thrall to this. The sacraments are 'merely seals or symbols of salvation and grace for believers', and therefore 'not absolutely necessary'.[191] Salvation is not dependent on these signs:

> if the sacrament is nothing but a seal, or rather a sort of symbol, it is not wrong for a man to have just as much trust in God, even without

---

189   Ibid., p. 500.
190   Ibid., p. 568.
191   Ibid., p. 556.

the seal, when it is not convenient for him to receive it properly. After all, he can give thanks to God and commemorate the death of Christ in many other ways every day of his life, even if he does not do so in the ceremonial way which God has instituted.[192]

It is better to steer clear of the eucharist, if it is being administered in an idolatrous way that implicates it in priestly power. There is no justification for insisting that only priests can preside: 'The early Christians are said to have taken part in it regularly and in their own homes . . . So I do not know why ministers should forbid anyone except themselves to celebrate the Lord's Supper.'[193] Are we not all equally priests in Christ? The eucharist is a new version of the Passover meal, at which the head of each family presided, rather than a priest. And the New Testament is supposed to have freed us from ritual rules, rather than brought new ones. 'Does it seem right that the head of a family, or anyone appointed by him, should not now be at liberty to distribute the Lord's Supper to his dependants, as he once distributed the passover?'[194]

Baptism is another sign that is not absolutely necessary. It should be understood as a vow taken by adult believers. Infant baptism is therefore a nonsense. Like the eucharist, the rite should be de-clericalized. To baptize another Christian takes no magic power: if 'any believer can preach the gospel, so long as he is endowed with certain gifts, it follows that any believer can administer baptism, because baptism is less important than the preaching of the gospel . . .'[195]

All Christians have a priestly function, yet the Gospel is especially reliant on prophets, apostles, evangelists, and others who spread the Word 'by preaching and by writing.'[196] Of course he places himself here: back in 1641 he had said that a great national poet has a moral and religious function, 'beside the office of a pulpit'.[197]

---

192   Ibid., p. 557.
193   Ibid.
194   Ibid., p. 558.
195   Ibid., p. 573.
196   Ibid., p. 570.
197   Milton, *The Reason of Church Government*, p. 816–17.

His section on the Bible shows that Milton was deeply suspicious of theology. Like Luther, he attacks the tradition of overlaying scripture with theory. Even Protestants tend to 'shroud [the scriptures] in the thick darkness of metaphysics.'[198] We are free to interpret scripture for ourselves: 'no visible church, then, let alone any magistrate, has the right to impose its own interpretations upon the consciences of men as matters of legal obligation, thus demanding implicit faith.'[199] If believers disagree over interpreting the Bible, 'they should tolerate each other until God reveals the truth to all.'[200] No form of church has intrinsic authority: 'it is not the visible church but the hearts of believers which, since Christ's ascension, have continually constituted the "pillar and ground of the truth."'[201] Anyone who tries to tell Christians what to believe, 'whether he acts in the name of the church or of a Christian magistrate, he is placing a yoke not only upon man but upon the Holy Spirit itself.'[202] If the apostles were right to reject the law, 'much less can any modern church . . . impose rigid beliefs upon the faithful.'[203] It follows from the Pauline principle of freedom from the law that Christians are free from any form of institutional orthodoxy.

Soon he comes to his ultimate bugbear: tithes. It is disgraceful for a minister to claim a right to parishioners' money: 'This sort of thing does not go on in any reformed church except ours.'[204] There's a lazy assumption that a priest has the right to rule over a parish, and receive public money. Milton proceeds in Thatcherite vein. ' "How are we to live then?" you may ask. How are you to live! Why, as the prophets and the apostles used to live, by making use of your own abilities, by some trade or some respectable profession. Follow the example of the prophets; they were quite accustomed to chop wood and build their own houses . . .'[205]

198   Milton, *De Doctrina Christiana*, p. 580.
199   Ibid., p. 584.
200   Ibid.
201   Ibid., p. 589.
202   Ibid., p. 590.
203   Ibid.
204   Ibid., p. 599.
205   Ibid., p. 599–600.

Each congregation of Christians, however small, is sovereign: it 'has no man, no assembly, and no convention on earth set over it, to which it is rightfully subject.'[206] No overarching institution is needed to 'oversee' them (the root meaning of episcopacy). Here Christianity breaks with Judaism, in which all the synagogues looked to the central event of Temple-worship. There is no analogous central event in Christianity: 'now everything that has to do with the worship of God and the salvation of believers, everything, in fact, that is necessary to constitute a church may be performed in a correct and properly ordered way in a particular church, within the walls of a private house where no great number of believers are assembled.'[207] Once again he is returning to the original New Testament model, and dissenting from the institutional revolution that transformed Christianity in the second and third centuries.

Each congregation is free to find its own style of worship, for there is no binding blueprint: 'Even the Lord's Prayer is a pattern or model, rather than a formula to be repeated verbatim either by the apostles or by the churches today. So it is clear that the church has no need of a liturgy: those who prompt and assist our prayers are divine helpers, not human.'[208] Milton hates the idea of idolizing a particular verbal convention. It might seem surprising that such an ardent a lover of language shunned the Prayer Book, but for Milton its sonorous beauty was always outweighed by theological principle. The lovely language lulled one into forgetting the danger of compromise with Rome. Milton's attitude is a good antidote to today's trite nostalgia for Prayer Book worship, the boring wistful consensus that we are losing our heritage. Instead of mourning tradition's erosion we are called to trust God, who delivers truth and beauty fresh each day. He is not bound to some noble verbal monument: he is in love with our capacity for improvisation, for making it new.

Milton's antinomianism is particularly striking in relation to the Sabbath. The idea of an especially holy day is superstitious nonsense. It is part of the Jewish law that the Gospel does away with – indeed the sacred

---

206   Ibid., p. 601.
207   Ibid., p. 602.
208   Ibid., p. 670.

is no longer tied to any particular time or place. Christians who appeal to the Ten Commandments falsely assume that 'the decalogue [is] a faultless moral code.'[209] In this instance it clearly ordains the old cultic law. And should not such legalists stick to the idea that the Sabbath is the seventh day of the week, rather than shifting it to the first? The Christian Sabbath is a muddle. Here Milton shows his disdain for mainstream Puritanism, which elevated the Sabbath to new importance. Indeed sabbatarianism was a key tool in the Puritans' attempt at social revolution: as we saw, James had issued his *Book of Sports* to counter sabbatarian zeal. His anti-sabbatarianism is good proof that Milton was the very opposite of a Puritan: he hated the idea of a pseudo-Christian law being imposed by bossy zealots. The Puritan desire for a 'godly' society was in large part a reversion to Jewish legalism. As he knew from his friend Henry Vane, the Sabbath was meticulously observed in Massachusetts. The city on a hill sounded to Milton like the city from hell.

De Doctrina Christiana, like all of Milton's religious thought, is a combination of 'back to Paul' and 'on to secular liberalism.'

My theological agreement with Milton is not complete. I think he might have been over-hasty in dispensing with the Trinity, in letting himself seem like a forerunner of deism. He seems too keen to apply his cherished principle: 'custom without truth is but agedness of error.' But I do not agree with those who think this puts him beyond the pale of true Christians. He did not exactly have a low opinion of Jesus Christ. I think it's more dubious to fetishize 'doctrinal orthodoxy' than to question it. Also, my wife will be relieved to hear that I do not share his enthusiasm for polygamy, or his sexism (he upholds Paul's decree that women should not speak in church). I find his whole approach to doctrine rather contradictory. His main point, it seems to me, is that doctrine should not be taken too seriously – we should get away from the idea that a 'real' Christian has to subscribe to certain quasi-philosophical formulae. Yet on the other hand, he insists on certain eccentric doctrines with crankish determination, and gives posterity an excuse to dismiss his theology. But some of his revisionary approach is before its time:

---

209   Ibid., p. 711.

his insistence that body and soul are inseparable anticipates recent philosophy and theology. In a confused and fallible way he is trying to get modern theology moving.

As the nation awaited, Charles II there was a widespread mood of excitement and relief, from lesser souls than Milton: a desire for life to get back to normal. Public opinion returned to its traditional royalism, which had never been far from the surface. Charles I was now officially the martyr rather than the war criminal. Clarendon was soon to write the official version, calling the regicide 'the most execrable murder that ever was committed since that of our blessed Saviour'.[210]

Charles's arrival, on May 25, was greeted by a few days of carnival. There was a lot of ostentatious Maypole dancing and suchlike, to humiliate the suddenly impotent Puritans. And Milton's predictions of monarchy's effect on the culture quickly came true: it gave rise to a new spirit of swagger, style, conspicuous consumption. 'The Restoration did not so much restore an old cultural world as usher in a new era whose hedonism far exceeded anything that had been seen before the outbreak of the Civil War. At the centre of this world was a libertine court – a society of Restoration rakes given more to drinking, gambling, swearing and whoring than to godliness – presided over by the King himself and his equally rakish brother, James, Duke of York'.[211]

Just before his arrival the new king had made a declaration promising to grant 'a Liberty to tender Consciences'. But this intention was swamped by a tide of jingoism that was expressed in popular hostility to sectarians: Baptist and Quaker meetings were attacked. Those associated with the old regime were of course in danger. Milton kept a very low profile: in November he was briefly imprisoned, but no charges were brought. Royalist retaliation was largely confined to the MPs who had authorized the regicide: Vane was arrested.

The Church of England was restored, of course: the question was whether a Presbyterian fringe should be tolerated, or whether uniformity

---

210 Edward Hyde, Earl of Clarendon, *The History of the Great Rebellion*, ed. by Roger Lockyer, Oxford University Press 1967, p. 455; p. 458.
211 Tim Harris, *Restoration: Charles II and his Kingdoms*, London: Penguin 2005, p. 48.

should be strictly imposed. The king's advisers urged him to the latter course: the series of laws known as the Clarendon Code established a tight religious monopoly, excluding dissenters from public life. Presbyterianism was outlawed, despite the fact that it had always been more royalist than republican. In 1661, the 'Cavalier Parliament' was elected; it was dominated by the Anglican squirearchy – the very last people to listen to Milton's theories about tithes.

His warnings against monarchy in *A Readie and Easy Way* proved pretty accurate. The court was Francophile, and Catholic-leaning. The king had a string of Catholic mistresses, and it was soon common knowledge that his brother, and heir, was a Catholic. The situation was very similar to that of the 1630s: a Catholic-leaning monarchy was daring to ignore Protestant opinion. Had the long and painful revolution of the 1640s and 1650s achieved nothing?

He quietly brooded on England's failure, and sometimes dared to signal his attachment to 'the good old cause'. When Vane was executed in 1662, he contributed his sonnet to an underground book on the radical politician. He obviously had to be careful about publishing, or even voicing, his opinions. There was an upside to this: he could at last attend to the other aspect of his literary persona, and write the great poem he had been casually mentioning for decades.

In 1662, the king married a Portuguese Catholic, and began a long campaign to ease anti-Catholic discrimination, but Parliament was having none of it: Anglican uniformity was imposed with new rigidity, culminating in the Conventicles Act, banning non-Anglican religious meetings. For Milton, it was painfully ironic that the foremost advocate of toleration in public life was a Catholic-leaning king. How depressing that toleration was becoming cynically linked to a tacitly illiberal agenda.

His domestic life was eased by another marriage, in 1663. The presence of a new young wife caused friction with his three daughters, and relations were never repaired. He seems to have found his daughters a nuisance, preferring the company of a small group of young men. One of these was a bookish Quaker called Thomas Ellwood, whose nonconformity barred him from the universities, and led to spells of imprisonment. He was an admirer of James Nayler. Milton kept his distance from all organized religion. As one his first biographers, John Toland, writes: 'In the latter part of his life he was not a professed member of any particular sect among Christians; he frequented none of their assemblies, nor made use of their particular rites in his family.'[212] A recent biographer adds: 'not only after the Restoration but also during the Interregnum, there is no evidence of Milton's formal membership in any parish or congregation.'[213]

He also stayed in touch with Marvell, his former colleague and fellow poet. It was probably Marvell who kept him safe from prosecution in the first dangerous years of the Restoration. Marvell typified the rising 'Whig' ideology: calmly and reasonably progressive. Liberty can be pursued without revolutionary purism: gently does it. Milton's attitude to this was that of the Old Labour politician to his New Labour successor.

It was Ellwood who arranged Milton's temporary residence outside London during the plague of 1665. He returned to London in time to see, or feel, the great fire. A letter survives from this time in which he reassures a distant correspondent that he has survived the plague: '. . . by the blessing of God, who had prepared a safe place for me in the country, I am both alive and well. Let me not be useless, whatever remains for me in this life.'[214] The parable of the talents is till in his mind. This austere sense of purpose, of service, of gratitude, is central to Milton's greatness. As he had written at the very beginning of *De Doctrina*: 'In the whole life and estate of man the first duty is to be grateful to God and mindful of his blessings.'

What did his young friends think of him? They probably saw him as a relic of the radicalism of the previous generation, a bit like Tony Benn or Harold Pinter today. When he talked of the great epic he was completing, they were probably polite rather than genuinely enthusiastic. Could his dated radicalism really speak to a new cultural era, full of brave new fashions Milton had no inkling of? Would he be able to resist the urge to bang on about tithes? *Paradise Lost* was published in 1667, and to everyone's

---

212   Quoted in Rowse 1977, p. 283.
213   Barbara K. Lewalski, *The Life of John Milton: A Critical Biography*, Oxford: Blackwell 2000, p. 435.
214   Milton, Letter to Heimbach, quoted in Beer 2008, p. 307.

surprise (except perhaps its author's) it sold very well, and gradually became part of the cultural landscape. The old blind eccentric had some-how reinvented himself in retirement. He used the political reverse as an opportunity to get round to the epic that he had been planning since his early thirties. It is a remarkable example of versatility in adversity.

The Epics

> Of man's first disobedience, and the fruit
> Of that forbidden tree, whose mortal taste
> Brought death into the world, and all our woe,
> With loss of Eden, till one greater man
> Restore us, and regain the blissful seat,
> Sing heavenly Muse, that on the secret top
> Of Oreb, or of Sinai, didst inspire
> That shepherd, who first taught the chosen seed,
> In the beginning how the heavens and earth
> Rose out of chaos: or if Sion hill
> Delight thee more, and Siloa's brook that flowed
> Fast by the oracle of God: I thence
> Invoke thy aid to my adventurous song,
> That with no middle flight intends to soar
> Above the Aonian mount, while it pursues
> Things unattempted yet in prose or rhyme.

The genius of this opening sentence of *Paradise Lost* lies in the dullness of the first five lines, and the sudden release of energy at 'Sing'. This, incidentally, echoes my experience of the epic. When, as a teenager, I first heard of this text, it seemed dusty, dutiful, dull, a cold literary corpse that the other A-level set were unfortunate enough to have to dissect. I probably also got wind of some of the critical consensus on Milton too: this was a tedious bit of the canon that no one really wanted there, it seemed, but somehow refused to be budged. When I actually read the thing, at university – wow! The dullness fled and the 'Sing' sang. There is nothing like the force of that 'Sing' in all of English literature – a five line build-up to a one-word punch that turns the passage upside-down. The first three lines are particularly leaden. Indeed the first four words set the tone: after 'Of', two stresses – *man's first* – and then the awkward half-stress of *dis*-, leading to the very heavy stress of *-bed-*. One's just a few syllables into the poem, and it is already difficult, like wading through dark treacle, and one has to regain one's footing by putting huge stress on this grim word, *disobedience*. One practically has to shout it. And then in the next line there is a big stress on a similarly forbidding word: *forbidden*, and then on *mortal*, and then on *death*, and then on *woe*. It is almost parodically sombre. And then things lift a bit, with the reference to Christ restoring us, but the tone does not fully lift with the sense. This is partly because we are in a subordinate clause, in brackets almost. That is what makes the first five lines so heavily pregnant – we are dimly aware that we await a verb – we begin to need one, to thirst for the end of this clause, for the main meaning, and then, after this drumbeat of woe – *bang*: *Sing* – the first time a line starts with a stress. Here is the verb, and it is unexpectedly emphatic: an imperative. And only now do we really begin. Only now does the epic begin with the necessary energy. The first five lines are a trick. It is analogous to a public speaker pretending to stumble as he opens and then, with a brilliant joke, creating huge relief and excitement in his audience. This is a heavy, dull, serious theme, Milton faux-warns us, and then suddenly undoes the warning – relax, this is God's plot: is there in truth no beauty? 'Beauty' is too small a word: poetry brings energy, vitality, life. And a creative power that is best seen as *magical*. Suddenly we are out of the woods, free from the depressing abstractions of the first few lines, and we are in the fresh air of a landscape, a Claude Lorraine painting, with mountains and brooks and mythical figures. Poetry conjures this up. 'That shepherd' is Moses, who is traditionally seen as the author of Genesis, whose opening words are quoted. He is the shaman-storyteller, who re-creates creation. The original legislator is primarily a poet. 'Rose' is the second line-opening stress; it links the creation with the resurrection, and with the conjurer's power to raise spirits

Milton was fully blind now, and so felt his way into his mature persona. The great sonnet on his blindness was written around now. He returns to the parable of the talents, and wonders how he can fully serve God now, with this new handicap. He is tempted to complain at the unfairness, that his zeal to serve is so painfully frustrated, but the voice of Patience intervenes, telling him not to be so utilitarian. Serving God is not about delivering results, for he is beyond needing our achievements; it is about having the right attitude: 'who best / Bear his mild yoke, they serve him best.' One should know that God's will is far out of one's hands, and trust him. More than any other of Milton's poem, this one has an affinity with Herbert's poetry. In 'The Collar', for example, the speaker is beginning to rebel against God until a heavenly voice reassures him of his creaturely dependence. Blindness had a dual effect on him: it made him seem the austere prophet figure he had long felt himself to be, but it also softened him; it led him to foreground the idea of his childlike dependence on God. This is evident in a letter he wrote two years later to a physician friend; he wonders whether his condition is curable, and then wonders whether it matters: maybe man should 'find comfort in believing that he cannot see by the eyes alone, but by the guidance and wisdom of God. Indeed while He himself looks out for me and provides for me, which He does, and takes me as if by the hand, and leads me throughout life, surely, since it has pleased Him, I shall be pleased to grant my eyes a holiday.'[155] He came to see his blindness as a sort of war wound, a result of working so hard in the true cause. And this mellowed him, the sense that he had achieved something. He no longer had to be anxious about his rare calling: he had done his best, sacrificed himself, made a name for himself. In a sonnet to his friend Cyriack Skinner, he explains that he is consoled at the thought that he lost his sight 'In liberty's defence, my noble task, / Of which all Europe talks from side to side.' He has become a symbol; it satisfies him.

But he still had to contend with daily life, and it became harder when a double family tragedy struck: his wife died in labour, and shortly afterwards his son died. The frail domestic order he had so painfully acquired

---

155   Letter to Philaras, September 28, 1654, in CPW vol. 4 pt. 2, p. 870.

put down the deepest and most far-reaching roots in your souls,' it will be easily lost.

> Unless with true and sincere devotion to God and men . . . you drive from your minds the superstitions that are sprung from ignorance of real and genuine religion, you will have [new tyrants] . . . Unless you expel avarice, ambition, and luxury from your minds, yes, and extravagance form your families as well, you will find at home and within that tyrant, who, you believed, was to be sought abroad and in the field – now even more stubborn. In fact, many tyrants, impossible to endure, will from day to day hatch out from your very vitals. Conquer them first. This is the warfare of peace, these are its victories, hard indeed, but bloodless, and far more noble than the gory victories of war.[154]

The nation, to be truly free, must be a sort of mega-church. The idea of the public sphere must be secular in the sense of devoid of religious institutional power, but not secular in the sense of unreligious. Its culture must be enthusiastically Christian, in order to propagate this narrative of liberty's dependence on inner struggle. Of course Milton is influenced by Roman republican virtue, and Stoicism, as historians such as Quentin Skinner underline, but this supplements rather than replaces Christianity. We need a new sort of Christian state that draws on classical republican idealism, but is also – and primarily – rooted in the liberal Protestant tradition. It is Protestantism that enables us to separate church and state and so emulate classical republicanism.

In reality, the republic was becoming harder to defend. The battle for toleration was being lost. The tide had turned against the frail toleration of Biddle's Socinian views. Owen had successfully rallied the conservatives and the book was banned, and Biddle was formally prosecuted. There were calls for his mutilation, but Cromwell managed to get him banished to the Isle of Wight.

---

154   Ibid., p. 680–1.

(Milton is anti-Faustus). The next line-opening stress is 'Fast', and this encapsulates the turn-around since 'Sing'. The poem has sped up, it has been carried along by some force. That is the main point of the entire opening sentence: to perform divine inspiration. It finally introduces an element of risk: 'adventurous', 'unattempted yet'. There is a bit of showmanship here: it sounds like the patter of a magician or juggler: for the first time ever, ladies and gentlemen . . . *six balls!* That could be the poster slogan: 'unattempted yet in prose or rhyme'. Hold on to your hats: drum roll please.

> And chiefly thou O Spirit, that dost prefer
> Before all temples the upright heart and pure,
> Instruct me, for thou know'st . . .

I remember when I first read these lines. I remember the black words on the white page looking particularly clean, sharp, pure. I remember thinking something along the lines of: he is serious. He means it. This is not someone trying to look serious through a decorous old epic style. There is also an evangelical immediacy. 'Before all temples': Milton's theology is summed up here. No form of public religion is really trustworthy. There is more truth in the spirit of religious criticism, of defiant suspicion. Even as he criticizes religion, Milton is at his most priestly – it is a sort of virtual liturgy, especially when the poet now asks the Spirit to guide him. The poem is a sort of virtual church, a common space, accessible to godly individuals (and students of literature).

Of course Milton foregrounds himself. Is he not like Moses? In this epic, says Lewalski, 'Milton constructs his Bardic self in collaboration with his "heavenly Muse" in four extended Proems whose length and personal reference are without precedent in earlier epics.'[215]

This prayer to the Holy Spirit concludes with the famous words, 'That . . . I may assert eternal providence, / And justify the ways of God to men.' Modern critics enjoy showing how bravely free-thinking they are

215   Lewalski 2000, p. x.

by disputing his success. The God of the epic is just as horrid as the God of the Bible, they say. In a sense 'justify' justifies such a response. The claim to prove God's justice is bound to provoke angry heckling. It is a confrontational mission statement. Of course there can be no objective judgement as to Milton's apologetic success. For me, this text adds to the appeal of Christian faith; for many it confirms it the repulsiveness of that faith. Yet it should be noted that on one level his success is beyond dispute. This poem keeps the Christian story alive in a pocket of culture that is not overly sympathetic to it. Milton has forced literary modernity to reckon with this narrative. In the same way that the Noah story has wormed its way into the iconography of childhood, the Eden story is part of literary culture. In a sense, this achievement becomes more obvious the more de-Christianised our culture becomes. Because of Milton, today's literary critics who generally scorn religion are less free to ignore this stuff about good and evil, Satanic temptation, divine authority. Most of them will be coolly detached from the question of its truth, but they will still be engaging with it, keeping it current, like a lot of children playing with their wooden pairs of animals.

The poem is about the conflict between good and evil, which, in Christianity, means the victory of good over evil. This conflict takes the form of Satan's rebellion against God – which is the origin of our condition. It is clear from the start (as we have seen) that good triumphs over evil. But at the very heart of the poem is what seems to be evil's victory over good: the sullying of innocence.

The back-story, we quickly learn, is the 'foul revolt' of Satan against 'the throne and monarchy of God' (Bk.1: l.42). Monarchy, eh? Some critics make the laughable mistake of thinking that Milton the republican must harbour some sort of opposition, of the unconscious variety perhaps, towards the absolute monarch of heaven. The whole point is the opposite: he wants to show that his republicanism is rooted in his form of religious absolutism. God alone is the absolutely authoritative ruler, criticism of whom is sinful. He has already raised this idea in his prose. In *A Defence of the English People*, he dealt with his opponent's claim that Christ is a sort of king, being descended from royal stock, and that monarchy is therefore worthy of reverence. This does not follow, says

Milton. There is an absolute distinction between worldly kingship and Christ's kingship, which 'we recognize, it brings us joy, and we pray for his speedy advent: for he is worthy and there is none like him or resembling him. But, until that time, we are right in believing that to entrust the royal sway to men unworthy and undeserving, as has mostly been the case, has brought mankind more harm than good.'[216] Kingship belongs to theology not politics.

For a fervent republican to hymn divine monarchy is only incongruous if you forget the distinction between God and man, time and eternity. The main aim of *Paradise Lost* is the total re-location of kingly authority in God. Milton wants to show that this is the foundation of his political and religious vision, which is anti-authoritarian in worldly terms only. Similarly, he wants to show that his belief in liberty is not a general, abstract matter, but rooted in the Christian narrative: without this foundation, the pursuit of liberty will end in tears (and the restoration of monarchs). So in his retirement from public life Milton is going back to basics, setting out the full scale of his vision. It is wrong to think that he has turned away from his revolutionary creed, gone quietist. For his revolutionary creed had always been bigger than politics as it is understood by the modern secular mind. It had always been rooted in faith in God's eschatological revolution, his bringing of history's climax. Although he had used eschatological rhetoric to herald the parliamentary cause and then Cromwell's regime, he had not been so rash as to identify these movements with the Second Coming. He was not a secular utopian, who thought that the right sort of politics could perfect the world. So his motivation for writing *Paradise Lost* was not to forge a new, otherworldly hope, once his political god had failed. It was to clarify what he had always believed: that the true cause is founded on this myth. The truest revolutionary act is to re-tell this story, infect human culture with it.

In the first two books, we meet Satan, and his cronies. Satan presents himself as a freedom-fighter, down on his luck, defiant. He calls a council: the plotting demons sound like employees whinging about the boss, imagining their resentments are urgent and righteous. There is lots of

---

216   Milton, *A Defence of the English People*, p. 367.

brave rhetoric: for example Mammon urges his colleagues to prefer 'Hard liberty before the easy yoke / Of servile pomp' (2.255–6). A plot is agreed: to ruin God's new creation, man. Satan volunteers to investigate: this is a project that no 'difficulty or danger could deter / Me from attempting' (2.459–50); he embraces the 'hazard'. Soon 'Satan inflamed with thoughts of highest design, / Puts on swift wings, and towards the gates of hell / Explores his solitary flight . . .' (2.630–2). He is doing something adventurous, and unattempted yet. The echo of the poet's initial mission statement is clear. Yes, says Milton, there is an affinity between me, as poet, and Satan. So help me God. The difference is that the poet seeks to serve God, and is wary of the pride his job entails. In the introductory passage, he has asked the Spirit to 'raise and support' what is low in him: to deliver him from evil.

Satan is somewhat sympathetic. There's something dashing about his over-the-top pride, a sort of theatrical charm. And we warm to his underdog quality: as Wain says, 'defeat is the only thing that can make pride beautiful.'[217] But his attractiveness should not be overstated. Many critics imply that the balance of the epic is upset by the force of Satan's personality. It seems that such critics choose to accentuate the charm of Satan, for whatever reason. The stronger charm is in the innocence of Adam and Eve, and the drama of their error.

It goes without saying, or ought to, that a poetic depiction of a conversation between God and his Son is unlikely to be entirely satisfactory, either aesthetically or theologically. This is what Milton offers in the first half of Book Three. It feels like a medieval Mystery Play, in which a character comes on, doing God in a stiff, authoritative way. The fall and rise of man is predicted, and angelic celebrations ensue, which feel lifelessly orderly. One just has to get through this part of the poem. The reader is grateful to rejoin Satan, on his great adventure, his sci-fi odyssey through the cosmos.

Of course this is Milton's intention, that the reader is attracted to the dynamism of Satan, and inclined to take his side against God, to agree that he is a celestial bully. Stanley Fish has rightly chided critics who 'end

---

217   In Kermode 1960, p. 5.

by accusing God or by writing volumes to expose the illogic of His ways.'[218] In the world of the poem, God's absolute goodness, as well as absolute power, is simply a fact. To argue otherwise is to echo Satan's logic. As Fish says, Milton means to nudge us towards seeing it Satan's way, and (ideally) to notice this with alarm, and be more conscious of our fallibility: 'Submitting to the style of the poem is an act of self-humiliation . . . By accepting the challenge of self-criticism and self-knowledge, one learns how to read, and by extension how to live, and becomes finally the Christian hero who is, after all, the only fit reader.'[219]

The epic really comes to life once we get to Eden: all the introductory hell scenes are really for inferno-nerds. It is only now, when Satan spies on the primal pair, that the narrative becomes fully psychologically and theologically profound. Indeed the scene that now unfolds is utterly unique. We are suddenly looking at perfect innocence, and we are sharing the gaze of perfect evil. It is all so idyllic, so childlike, so, pure, that our impulse is to sneer with Satan, to want it pulled down. Eve is a perfect naked beauty, who 'as a veil down to the slender waist / Her unadorned golden tresses wore / Dishevelled, but in wanton ringlets waved / As the vine curls her tendrils . . .' She has sexy hair – but it does not impinge on her purity. Indeed it soon emerges that she enjoys sex, but pre-lapsarian sex is utterly innocent. We cannot imagine this innocence: when we try to, we turn it dirty. Yet Milton is forcing us to try to! If the depiction of their tender lovemaking seems softly pornographic, the fault lies in the reader, whose response is clouded by lust. It is the most amazingly daring bit of writing. As they sit together at the end of the day, Eve, 'half embracing leaned / On our first father, half her swelling breast / Naked met his under the flowing gold / Of her loose tresses hid . . .' (4.494–7). They kiss, and Satan is filled with envious rage at the sight of 'these two / Imparadised in one another's arms.' He flies off, unable to watch. But we stay: we hear them discuss the beauty of the evening, then retire to their 'blissful bower'. The reader's impatient interest is gently rebuked: before they enter their dwelling, both 'under open sky adored / The God that made both sky, air,

---

218   Stanley Fish, *Surprised by Sin: The Reader in Paradise Lost*. London: Macmillan 1997, p. 272.
219   Ibid., p. 207.

earth and heaven / Which they beheld, the moon's resplendent globe /
And starry pole . . .' (4.721–4). Yes yes, get on with it. They voice their
thanks, 'and other rites / Observing none, but adoration pure / Which
God likes best, into their inmost bower / Handed, they went.' Soon we
hear that Eve does not refuse 'the rites / Mysterious of connubial love.' It
is a religious act. In fact, wedded love is a banishing of lust (4.753–4), and
of the whole culture of pagan eroticism (4.767–70). Of course this is the
very heart of the poem: the innocent sensual happiness that the reader
can only imagine with an effort that exposes his fallenness.

The decision to depict their lovemaking is obviously a daring one,
verging on sacrilege. St Augustine had long ago speculated on Edenic sex.
It probably did not happen, he thought. If it had happened, of course it
would have been pure. But it is a mistake to try to imagine it.

> We are speaking of something which is *now* a matter of shame; and
> therefore, though we conjecture as best we can what it would have
> been like before it became shameful, it is very necessary that our dis-
> course be rather reined in by modesty than assisted by eloquence . . .
> [H]ow when mention is made of it *now* can it be presented to human
> fantasy except in the likeness of the turbid lust we have tried and not
> of the tranquil volition we conjecture?[220]

C. S. Lewis is inclined to agree that Milton took a risk too far: 'the poet
hardly seems to be aware of the magnitude of his own undertaking. He
seems to . . . hope that when he writes "half her breast Naked met his" we
shall be able, without further assistance, to supply for Adam an experi-
ence both very like and totally unlike anything that a fallen man could
possibly enjoy!'[221] But surely this is the point, that the reader will be
ambiguously excited by the pure sex. He will (if sufficiently pious) yearn
for the innocence, and he also will (if sufficiently human) turn it into soft
porn. In a sense this is sacrilegeous: Milton allows Adam and Eve to

---

220 Augustine, *De Civitatis* XIV, 26, quoted in C. S. Lewis, *A Preface to Paradise Lost*. Oxford
     University Press, London 1960, p. 122.
221 Ibid., p. 124.

become sex objects. Yet it is in a good cause: the reader's acknowledgement of his fallenness. Milton is using poetry's creative magic to conjure up heaven – the form of heaven we have a half-buried ability to imagine. And he is simultaneously alerting us to the painful otherness of it, which is to say our sinfulness. Interestingly, this idea of Christian poetry is already present in the Elizabethan theorist Philip Sidney, quoted earlier. The magic of poetry may be seen as a proof of the doctrine of the fall, for 'our erected wit maketh us know what perfection is, and yet our infected will keepeth us from reaching into it.'[222] Poetry, as well as delighting us, can nurture that necessary tension, that awareness of our exile. Maybe Sidney's observation was the seed of *Paradise Lost*.

Satan is incapable of sex; he can only desire. He can't get no satisfaction. Humanity, in its pristine state, is therefore defined by successful, pleasurable sex. Indeed their sex is better than we can entirely imagine. We have another chance to try, in Book 8, when Adam tells the angel Raphael of their first lovemaking. Milton's genius is to dare to foreground sex, to make it so theologically loaded. The (male) reader identifies with Adam, viscerally, bodily. He also tells Raphael of being in love with her. He struggles to reconcile this with the fact that he has been told that she is his inferior. This is the most powerful little description of a man's love for a woman that I know of.

> . . . when I approach
> Her loveliness, so absolute she seems
> And in herself complete, so well to know
> Her own, that what she wills to do or say,
> Seems wisest, virtuousest, discreetest, best;
> All higher knowledge in her presence falls
> Degraded, wisdom in discourse with her
> Looses discountenanced, and like folly shows;
> Authority and reason on her wait,
> As one intended first, not after made . . .

(8.546–56)

---

222 Sidney 1965, p. 101.

His love makes him feel weak, it blurs the gender hierarchy of Eden. Is Milton saying that female attractiveness is dangerous? No: despite what happens, this is the natural divine order of things, and God's greatest gift to Adam. Raphael replies in strangely irrelevant terms, saying in effect that sex is a biological urge, and that he should not overestimate what all animals do. He explains that angels have a form of spiritual sex with each other, a sort of post-carnal air-sex (as angels seem to be all-male, are they therefore homosexual?). It seems that angels are existentially ignorant.

Traditionally the Fall is Eve's fault, and telling the story is a way of justifying female subservience – but Milton actually seems to question this misogyny in his narrative. As Anna Beer says, after the fall, 'Milton tries to make the reader understand the reasons for her actions and demonstrates her quiet heroism.'[223] (She also notes that earlier on Milton seems to be 'reclaiming female sexuality as a positive thing'.[224]) The fallen humanity of the pair is very vivid. Milton repeats his trick of foregrounding sex. They have a sweaty, torrid, drugged-up embrace after which the full horror of their estrangement from bliss becomes apparent. (I disagree with C. S. Lewis, who says that Milton 'has made the unfallen [sex] already so voluptuous and kept the fallen still so poetical that the contrast is not so sharp as it ought to have been.'[225]) Once they fall they suddenly acquire a new level of psychological credibility – though they have already been fully engaging in their innocent state – which gives the epic a second wind.

The final books sketch the Christian vision. There is repeated emphasis on the conflict between God and Satan, the epic battle between them. Satan seems to have won the first round, but God will use this setback to produce a larger-scale victory. God tells the serpent that the woman's seed shall 'bruise thy head' – this verse from Genesis is traditionally understood to refer to Christ's victory over Satan. This is the core theology of *Paradise Lost* (and, as we shall see, *Paradise Regained*): an assertion of the cosmically victorious Christ, known in Christian tradition as 'Christus Victor'. In fact it is first unfolded in Book 3, by Christ himself:

223   Beer 2008, p. 334.
224   Ibid., p. 325.
225   Lewis 1960, p. 70.

following his sacrificial death, he says, 'I shall rise victorious, and subdue / My vanquisher, spoiled of his vaunted spoil; / Death his death's wound shall then receive . . ' (3.250–53). When Adam and Eve have fallen, this is the key message that they are given. Satan is going down. Knowledge of this drama, this triumphant divine violence, is Christian faith. After Adam tries praying, he tells Eve, 'peace returned / Home to my breast, and to my memory / His promise, that thy seed shall bruise our foe; / Which . . . / Assures me that the bitterness of death / Is past, and we shall live' (11.153–8). In the final book, the Archangel Michael gives Adam and Eve a preview of religious history. The essence of the lesson is this same image. God will reveal himself to the Jews, 'informing them, by types / And shadows, of that destined Seed to bruise / The Serpent, by what means he shall achieve / Mankind's deliverance' (12.232–35). Soon they are told that Jesus 'shall quell / The adversary serpent, and bring back / Through the world's wilderness long wandered man/ Safe to eternal paradise of rest' (12.311–14). How is Jesus' victory actually won, asks Adam excited? 'By fulfilling that which thou didst want [lack], / Obedience to the law of God' (12.396–7). Christ's death and resurrection 'Shall bruise the head of Satan, crush his strength, Defeating Sin and Death, his two main arms, / And fix far deeper in his head their stings / Than temporal death shall bruise the victor's heel' (12.428–33).

Christ's followers will be strengthened by the Spirit, and so 'able to resist/ Satan's assaults, and quench his fiery darts' (12.491–2). Christian culture will become corrupted (significantly, Milton doesn't use the word 'church'). 'Wolves shall succeed for teachers, grievous wolves . . ' (12.508). They will pervert the Gospel with superstition and legalism; they will 'join / Secular power, though feigning still to act / By spiritual, to themselves appropriating / The Spirit of God, promised alike and giv'n / To all believers . . . What will they then / But force the Spirit of Grace itself, and bind / His consort Liberty . . .?' (12.516–26). The warning of wolves reminds us of the 'blind mouths' of 'Lycidas'. It is worth noting the consistency of Milton's vision. Also, the Christus Victor theme reminds us of an even earlier poem, the Nativity Ode. From his student days to his last days, he is concerned to trumpet the very essence of the Christian message: the power of Christ over all evil. In his middle years he became more focused on applying this vision to the politics of his day, and sharpening it, but this does not affect the consistency. The narrative of political excitement followed by crushing disappointment is massively overstated: he was consistently loyal to this cosmic vision.

In the Introduction, I mentioned that, despite lots of good critical work on *Paradise Lost* in recent decades, the cliché of God-the-authoritarian-baddie abides. The chief cliché-monger of our time is the popular novelist Philip Pullman, whose series of books *His Dark Materials* was inspired by the poem, as he explains:

> I found that my interest was most vividly caught by the meaning of the temptation-and-fall theme. Suppose that the prohibition on the knowledge of good and evil were an expression of jealous cruelty, and the gaining of such knowledge an act of virtue? Suppose the Fall should be celebrated and not deplored? As I played with it, my story resolved itself into an account of the necessity of growing up, and a refusal to lament the loss of innocence. The true end of human life, I found myself saying, was not redemption by a nonexistent Son of God, but the gaining and transmission of wisdom . . . This is how one modern writer told this great story.[226]

What is one to say to this? He seems to believe that he is retelling the same story as Milton told, despite putting trite humanism in the place of theology. It is no longer *this* story if you get rid of its stated objective: the communication of divine authority.

Paradise Lost is uniquely critic-proof. If someone announces that the epic fails in its intention, he is rebuked by the possibility that it is him who has failed to be one of the 'fit yet few' readers whom Milton hopes for. It is not trying to be a standard work of literature, but a religious communication.

On another level, it is a miraculous literary creation: these other worlds are given sudden new definition, substance, in a way that feels

---

226   Philip Pullman, Introduction to *Paradise Lost, an Illustrated Edition*, Oxford: Oxford University Press 2005, p. 10.

magical. C. S. Lewis has it just right: 'The marvel about Milton's Paradise or Milton's Hell is simply that they are there – that the thing has at last been done – that our dream stands before us and does not melt.'[227]

The boldness and power with which Milton depicts the Fall is really beyond the ability of literary criticism to express. It is a completely unique bit of writing; there is nothing to compare it to. Well, almost nothing. There is a similar spirit in Blake's *Songs of Innocence and Experience*: for here too we are confronted with the gulf between purity and dirty knowledge. Blake learned from Milton to apply his prophetic style to the immanent Fall, the gulf between our best and worst attitudes. And I also see a (less direct) parallel in Nabokov's novel *Lolita*. For it forces us to confront the adult's exile from natural goodness, as well as childhood innocence, and our terrible attraction to witty evil. The voice of Humbert Humbert seduces its style-loving readers, makes Eves of them.

Humbert's resemblance to Satan is foregrounded at the beginning of Chapter Thirteen.[228] The narrator comes downstairs in his pyjamas and dressing-gown and finds his landlady's twelve-year-old daughter bunking church. A playfight is twisted into a masturbatory cuddle; a dressed rehearsal for the full-scale seduction to come. The scene is peppered with references to *Paradise Lost*. We are meant to associate our witty narrator with the Prince of Darkness himself. There are some rather obvious hints, including the fact that the tussle begins over the 'Eden-red apple' Lolita is eating, and the fact that Humbert 'slipped on a purple silk dressing gown'; he is a cliché of louche evil. He also tells us that his surreptitious act of self-gratification sets 'all paradise loose.'

A subtler reference to Eden comes right at the start of the chapter. When he emerges from his room he 'crept to the banisters' in his slippers in order to eavesdrop on a conversation between Lolita and her mother. The creeping and eavesdropping are quiet allusions to Book Nine of *Paradise Lost*, in which Satan takes on snakey form in order to spy on Eden. Earlier on he has explained that, to be a lover of young girls, 'You have to be an artist and a madman, a creature of infinite melancholy,

227 Lewis 1960, p. 58.
228 Vladimir Nabokov, *Lolita*, London: Penguin (1955), 1980, p. 56ff.

with a bubble of hot poison in your loins and a super-voluptuous flame permanently aglow in your subtle spine (oh, how you have to cringe and hide!) . . .' In *Paradise Lost*, Satan conceals himself in the 'bestial slime' of the snake with a sort of defiant disgust at himself. He almost exults in the vileness as a proof of his passion. He, who was the highest of the angelic spirits, must stoop to this absurd crudity in the pursuit of his singular desire. This is the essential pathos of Humbert. He requires our sympathy that his delicate 'old-world' sensibility must, because of its rare passion for nymphets, stoop so low. It is, he suggests, grimly comic that a person like him must pass for a dirty pervert. It is also tragic, the source of the extremest pathos. We are to have pity on him, as we laugh with him. In Chapter Five, he recounts how he learned to accept his sexual orientation. He tried to fight it, he assures us: 'One moment I was ashamed and frightened, another recklessly optimistic. Taboos strangulated me. Psychoanalysts wooed me with pseudoliberations of pseudolibidos.' These three sentences are good evidence of his rhetorical subtlety. His claim to have resisted the impulse becomes self-justification, self-congratulation at the defiance of taboos and pseudoscience. He goes on that his desire 'appeared to me at times as a forerunner of insanity. At other times I would tell myself that it was all a question of attitude, that there was really nothing wrong in being moved to distraction by girl-children.' In other words, 'Evil, be thou my good.' He is deciding to redefine good and evil according to his desire. The comedy masks the absoluteness of Humbert's evil, even as it acknowledges it. He uses endless religious language for comic effect. He tells us that for many years his pursuit of nymphets led only to a few awkward incidents, though 'some of them ended in a rich flavour of hell.' He nudges us towards agreeing that he is really the victim of his terrible urge, and that his acquaintance with 'hell' is no different from one's own. And when his seduction of Lolita begins there are constant funny references to himself as 'monster' or 'beast'. Such language poses as comic exaggeration – and works incredibly well as such – yet is also crucially *not* exaggeration but perfectly apt. It constantly encourages us to enjoy the humour and forget the aptness.

Humbert's rhetoric is scarily effective at disarming us morally, spiritually. It is almost impossible to remain soberly conscious of the horror of his crime, of the evil of his soul, for we are all the time grateful for his verbal magic. *Lolita* is a re-write of *Paradise Lost* in which the Satanic voice has slipped its meta-narrative moorings. It makes one share C. S. Lewis' concern: the author 'hardly seems to be aware of the magnitude of his own undertaking'. But maybe that's the mark of the very best writing. As Anna Beer says, the epic is 'a high-risk poem in which Milton, and his readers, confront their demons.'[229]

Paradise Regained is the difficult second epic. Its message is precisely what Michael told Adam about Christ: he defeats Satan through his heroic obedience. So we see Jesus in the wilderness, being tempted. The setting is relatively localized, ordinary: two characters arguing in the desert. This is the historical Jesus, at the beginning of his ministry: a young man pondering his calling. Yet in Milton's depiction he is almost as mythological as the infant of the Nativity Ode strangling snakes in the cradle. The humanity is very much subordinated to the cosmic victory theme. Like Paul, Milton always feels the need to emphasize the powerful, mythological, saving Christ over the historical Jesus.

It is fairly customary to call the work a failure, due to the psychological incredibility of Christ, the stiltedness of the action, and the relatively lackluster performance of Satan. There is less here for the religiously unsympathetic reader. One probably has to sympathise with the narrative of Jesus rebuking Satan, to see merit in the poem. It is Milton's least aesthetic and most religious major poem. It is an illustration of the power of the Word – the verbal force of God. Christ is depicted through his rhetorical style: calm, certain, unfazed (like the Lady in the masque). Milton contrasts this with the gushy falsity of Satan, who is not now as compelling a presence as he was in *Paradise Lost*. There is something obvious and clichéd about him, and he is no longer in control of the action's unfolding. We know more than him, about the identity of his adversary. Christ's rhetoric comes across as relatively dynamic, fresh. On the other hand, it is hard to ignore Christ's resemblance to Milton. He is a shy, proud bookish type, who does not quite seem cut out for a public ministry among peasants. He is a cross between a brilliant undergraduate and

229   Beer 2008, p. 315.

Superman. It is hard to dispute the judgement that Milton 'has no sense of the dangers inherent in so unqualified an identification between the Hero's righteousness and his own.'[230] When Belial advises Satan to tempt him with women, Satan instinctively knows that he is made of sterner stuff than to fall for mere women (maybe Milton is wary of writing 'The Last Temptation of Christ'). When he tries to seduce him with worldly fame, Christ / Milton has a rant about celebrity culture and the poor taste of the vulgar: the people are just 'a herd confused, / A miscellaneous rabble, who extol / Things vulgar . . .'(3.49–51).

Satan keeps offering new temptations, and his offers are soberly rebutted. The glories of classical civilization are turned down, as is the chance to be a Jewish revolutionary hero. He even turns down a lovely meal served by pretty boys. He is then offered the chance to reform the Roman Empire, make it a beacon of liberty. Its citizens are too enmired in effeminate luxury to be saved, says Christ. They fail to yearn for freedom (this is a side-swipe at the monarchy-loving English, of course). Christ's rejection of the Roman Empire seems to reflect Milton's growing doubts about the early stages of the British Empire. He seems to agree with St Augustine that imperialism is unjustifiable violence, veiled in idealistic rhetoric. Cromwell's imperialism seemed to have been different, for there was a genuine desire to spread liberty – but maybe this too was tainted. He hinted at a similar scepticism in *Paradise Lost*: Satan is motivated by the desire to colonise humanity; in his brave adventuring he resembles a conquistador, planting his flag in a new world (eg. 10.470ff). And of course Adam reacts with pacifist horror at his glimpse of Nimrod's usurpation of dominion (12.63ff). The desire to rule others is demonic. This is not to say that Milton has turned pacifist and advocates a withdrawal from Ireland, but he is at least raising the issue for reflection. Incidentally, Malcolm X foregrounded this aspect of *Paradise Lost*, which he read in prison: 'The devil, kicked out of paradise, was trying to regain possession. He was using the forces of Europe . . . I interpreted this to show that the Europeans were motivated and led by the devil . . .'[231]

---

230   W. W. Robson, 'The Better Fortitude', in Kermode 1960, p. 136.
231   Malcolm X, quoted in Tobias Gregory, 'Hero as Hero', *London Review of Books*, 6 March 2008, p. 17.

Rejecting Satan's offer of Roman rule, Christ speaks of his eventual assumption of power:

> Know therefore when my season comes to sit
> On David's throne, it shall be like a tree
> Spreading and overshadowing all the earth,
> Or as a stone that shall to pieces dash
> All monarchies beside throughout the world,
> And of my kingdom there shall be no end.

> (4.146–51)

There is a hint here that Milton is still not entirely closed to the Christian utopianism has long flirted with. The tree image sounds like a gradual process that creeps up on history, and the next image reminds us that the fall of worldly monarchies is to be expected.

One of the big question-marks of Christianity is how the Second Coming comes. Is it a sudden supernatural event at the very end of history, or is it a process that begins within history, that makes use of what we call progress? As we saw in Chapter 1, in relation to Luther, the Reformation brings thoughts of the Last Days to the fore. The fully pure Gospel is bound to provoke the forces of darkness into new aggression: history is in the home straight. Milton adapts this picture, linking it to the hope of a new era of liberty. Maybe the first stage in the coming of God's kingdom can be identified with the political cause of English liberty. But this should not be overstated: his hope for the revolution was not outright utopianism. As Barker says, 'the revolution ought to have resulted in a society, imperfect but progressing, in which good men should have been free to achieve fullness of life and to meditate upon divine truth.'[232] He never explicitly advocates a this-worldly utopian understanding of Christian hope. Indeed he often states a reasonably orthodox belief in a post-historical Second Coming.

Though he does not preach utopianism, he does want to open up the question of the relationship between the kingdom of God and human

---

232 Arthur Barker, *Milton and the Puritan Dilemma*, Toronto: University of Toronto Press, 1942, p. 331.

history. He has been tacitly wrestling with this question for decades, but it is now, in the epics, that it comes to the fore. As Lewalski says, the epics bring 'new emphasis on the nature of Christ's kingdom and of the difficulties of interpreting God's word and his action in history'.[233] For Milton, the cause of liberty is not just one movement within fallen history: it is closely related to God's liberation of history from demonic power. It is divinely ordained progress – perhaps even the means by which God brings his final rule. But the relationship between historical progress and the kingdom of God is elusive and frustrating: we can never be sure that a seeming advance will not be reversed, and on the other hand, God might use a seeming reverse to further his cause. We should remember that progress towards liberty is in God's hands. It is not an intelligible 'system'. It is not for us to know why England saw a partial, temporary triumph of liberty, and then reverted to its political errors, like a dog to its vomit. Of course Milton was disappointed by this, but his disappointment has been overstated by modern critics who assume that the only real hope is secular-political, and that once Milton lost this, he must have been in despair. In reality, his hope was always more supernatural and eschatological than political – from the Nativity Ode to the epics. But of course he had dared to hope on the political level as well, and this hope had been dashed. After 1660, he had to remember that political hope was inessential – something that might or might not be present. The Christian might have to live through an era of dark reaction. What mattered was Christian hope, which is beyond the success of any political cause: even if history goes horribly wrong, it remains possible and necessary to hope for God's eventual victory. So we must resist the assumption that there is a gulf between political hope and otherworldly religious hope; that Milton's epics express a withdrawal to religion. The fact is that he has always believed in the eschatological Second Coming, in God's miraculous consummation of history, *and* he has believed that the historical cause of liberty is God's will and somehow related to his

---

233   Lewalski 2000, p. xiii.

final plans. It is not an 'either-or': either historical hope or supernatural hope. Milton believes that the Christian is called to both hopes.

Samson Agonistes, his final epic poem, wrestles with this. It is about the struggle to deal with short-term disappointment, and to remember that long-term hope remains valid. Samson, says Belloc, 'is Milton in every particular – the man fallen upon evil times, the man gone blind, the man impoverished, the man disappointed in women – and their victim.'[234]

He is an angry middle-aged man, the famous champion of Jewish liberation who has fallen from grace. He has reason to rage: he has been betrayed by his wife, blinded and imprisoned – he is now a Philistine freak-show. His deepest source of angst is his sense of abandonment by God. The narrative of his life, that he is God's special warrior, has run into the sand: he is just any old loser. His identity has gone. It is not fair, he eloquently cries. It was God's will that he married a Philistine: it was part of God's plan to deliver Israel from her foes. And then he erred, by telling Delila the secret of his strength. Amid his rage he finds the wisdom to pray – to pray the prayer that Milton has often prayed: 'God, make me useful.' He begs God to 'turn / His labours, for thou canst, to peaceful end' (709). This is an important line: he wills peace, and is therefore re-grafted onto the story of God, who is ultimately, despite the violence that is to come, the God of peace. Delila visits him, and some unhappy domestic rhetoric follows. In contrast to *Paradise Lost*, sex is an unhappy business, and women are to blame. Sex has made Samson foolish, it has effeminized him. Then his Philistine rival Harapha arrives for some verbal sparring. Samson challenges him to a last fight, to see whose God is stronger, and through issuing the challenge he recovers his old confidence. He dares to voice a crazy faith that God might yet revive the narrative of his service. Summoned to the pagan sports-day of his enemies he at first refuses, then it occurs to him to agree. He pulls down the stadium, killing the flower of the enemy, a suicide-demolition-man terrorist. The mass destruction is a sort of apocalyptic orgasm – a figure of the

---

234 Belloc 1960, p. 272.

Second Coming. There is an echo of the Lady's threat to Comus, that her transmission of the Word will cause the earth to 'shake, / Till all thy magic structures, reared so high, / Were shattered into heaps o'er thy false head.'

Though it imitates Greek tragedy, the message of this poem is that God does not do tragedy. Samson seems the tragic hero, cut off from divine favour. But his prayer to be allowed to serve is granted. It is a dramatic exposition of the final line of the sonnet: 'They also serve who only stand and wait.' Patience and trust are vindicated. Their vindication might not be pretty, but it happens. Modern history is like the Old Testament: God will further his cause, in surprising ways. What look to us like terrible setbacks are details of an unknowably cunning plan. Despite historical disappointments, God will turn things around in strange and miraculous ways – ultimately he will put the world to rights, whether through smooth progress or rough violence.

It is hard to imagine Milton writing such great poems if the Commonwealth had lasted. He needed to be forced to take a step back from politics, in order to reflect on his deepest subject matter: supra-political hope, the struggle to have hope despite the course of history. There are grounds for thinking that he was half-expecting the dashing of his political hopes all along. Back in 1642, in *The Reason of Church Government*, he had said that part of a great national bard's role was 'to deplore the general relapses of kingdoms and states from justice and God's true worship.'[235] Even at this stage he was not a starry-eyed boy who thought that utopia was round the corner.

In recent years, critics have asked whether *Samson Agonistes* celebrates terrorism. Is Milton saying that a godly warrior has the right to kill himself, and many others, in a bloody act of faith? Basically, no: he is certainly not suggesting that Protestant nonconformists should come up with their own version of the Gunpowder Plot. What the critics who earnestly debate the point forget is that Milton was a Christian rather than a Jew, and that Christians affirm the Old Testament stories with a certain detachment, or irony. As we have seen Milton is very clear indeed that Christianity turns Judaism upside-down, that the old rules are repealed.

---

235   Ibid., p. 816–17.

He considered the holy warrior ethic of the Judges, their form of jihad, to be a stage in religious history that Christianity had moved on from – yet could still use as a mythological resource.

A very last tract

In 1672, the king made another attempt to mitigate Anglican uniformity, for the sake of making life easier for his Catholic friends. His ultimate hope was that he would be able to convert without provoking another civil war. Milton was disgusted at his self-serving claim to favour toleration. Yet on the other hand, he was no fan of the conservative Anglican lobby, which pressed for tighter uniformity (and succeeded in obtaining it). He still wanted what he had always wanted: real, principled toleration, which meant toleration for all Protestants. He was provoked into a final prose work, *Of True Religion*. To some, it is proof that his love of toleration was limited. Actually it is the opposite. Toleration is so crucial that it must be distinguished from a merely laissez-faire approach. English culture was flirting with relativism. All religion is much the same, so let us try tolerating everyone, including Catholics, and see what happens. No, said Milton: Protestantism has an inner affinity with liberalism that Catholicism lacks. If it is tolerated it will obscure that affinity between Protestantism and liberalism.

He begins by attacking the ideal of religious uniformity. What is wrong with various sects competing for adherents, a free market in religion? He notes that in Jesus' time the Pharisees and the Sadducees were two sects, 'yet both met together in their common worship of God at Jerusalem.'[236] It is shameful that Protestant sects are persecuted in England, a supposedly Protestant state, when such sects are often tolerated in Catholic states, notably France and Poland. What are we scared of? The spread of heresy? If Protestants are trying to worship God on the basis of scripture, they cannot be accused of heresy. Of course they are prone to error, as we all are: such error is part of truth-seeking. The only real heresy is to try

---

236   Milton, *Of True Religion*, CPW vol. 8, p. 422–3.

to impose a system that tramples on freedom of conscience and the authority of scripture: Roman Catholicism. But will not pluralistic Protestantism end in chaos? Milton's liberalism is dependent on trust:

> The Gospel commands us to tolerate one another, though of various opinions, and hath promised a good and happy event [outcome] thereof . . . St Paul judged that not only to tolerate, but to examine and prove [test] all things, was no danger to our holding fast to that which is good.[237]

Catholicism utterly lacks this spirit of liberal hope. It brings a sort of tragic pathos: life is grim, so let us have the strongest, most emotionally powerful medicine of salvation. It consoles you with 'confessions, absolutions, pardons, indulgences, Masses, Agnus Deis, relics and the like.'[238] If Catholicism returns, it will change our view of what religion is. It will seem like the strong medicine that we need. As we saw in his first polemics, Milton sees Catholicism as dangerously appealing. Protestantism often looks weak and flimsy beside it, like a thinning of Christianity. As we saw, he thinks of the English Church as still in love with Rome, in thrall to it. At the risk of sounding like Ian Paisley, there are grounds for thinking that Milton was right – though the danger he predicted was far in the future. In the nineteenth century, Catholicism was granted toleration, and soon the Church of England took a sharply Roman turn. When Catholicism is culturally central, it changes the general perception of what Christianity is. And that is indeed damaging for the old alliance of Protestantism and liberalism. Atheist secularists will naturally associate the repressive tendencies of Catholicism with Christianity in general.

Though many critics glibly chide his failure to tolerate Catholicism, Milton's approach anticipates the majority liberal view today. For example, in an interview the Liberal Democrat leader Nick Clegg was asked whether we should tolerate the 'profoundly intolerant forces in out society'. He replied:

---

237   Ibid., p. 436.
238   Ibid., p. 438.

Of course there are limits to tolerance, absolutely. When I say 'toler-ance', I don't mean relativism. I don't mean a sort of moral free-for-all. Far from it, actually. Liberalism – muscular liberalism – should be, and is, very antagonistic to creeds and ideologies that espouse an intolerant, narrow-minded approach to things. Personally I think that if you live in a liberal democracy there are certain ground rules that everyone has to respect: you know, human rights, respect for the individual, gender equality, democracy. If you explicitly flout or con-found those values, I think it's quite reasonable for a liberal democracy to say, 'You're not part of our moral discussion.'[239]

Islamic extremism has reminded us that liberalism has to be something more than a blank space, that it has to reject its opposite – this ought to make us sympathise with Milton's stand against Catholicism.

His final years seem to have been happy enough, despite nasty attacks of gout. According to Aubrey, 'he would be cheerful even in his Gowte-fitts; & sing.'[240] He enjoyed showing the stiffness of his upper lip, as ever. And he doubtless knew that his lifelong prayer, to be useful in God's service, had been granted.

He died in November 1674. He was buried in an Anglican church, St Giles', Cripplegate. His reputation grew and grew. In 1737, a monu-ment was erected in Westminster Abbey, the shrine of establishment. Of course it was his poetry rather than his prose that won him his place in the pantheon. Had he only written prose his influence would have been far more localized. It is possible to see his poetry as a sort of Trojan horse, which gets his entire oeuvre admitted into the inner places of church and state, in order to undermine them from within.

---

239   Nick Clegg, interview with Simon Barrow, *Third Way*, May 2008.
240   Aubrey, quoted in Lewalski 2000, p. 536.

Conclusion

There is something problematic about Milton's identity. We do not quite know what he is. A great poet, surely? But the label gets it a bit wrong, for the idea of poetic greatness has, since his death, kept moving in a direction that makes Milton look so eccentric. In the post-Romantic climate, a poet's thought is very much secondary to his art. In fact this climate probably began with Johnson. To call Milton a great poet is to collude in the marginalization of his religious and political vision. It is a bit like calling Jesus a great moral teacher. It sounds like praise, but it overlooks what Milton was claiming to be – a prophet of the true religious and political cause. A purely literary-critical response to Milton is a sort of arrogance: it tacitly claims that inconvenient ideas can be put to one side, while his worth is assessed. (Is 'Literature' a way of avoiding religious ideas?) Of course the contemporary literary critic takes an interest in Milton's thought, but as background. What if it is the foreground? What if the really important question is not what we think of his poetry but what we think of his ideas? What if our most important religious thinker is buried under 'a great poet'. There is something wrong with the fact that Milton is studied in literature departments. It exposes a larger wrongness about our intellectual culture, our nervous evasion of ideas, especially religious ones.

As the reader might have noticed by now, I am a fan of his ideas. It seems to me that his fusion of Protestantism and liberalism is something we need to learn from. Of course he was not the only influential liberal Protestant thinker of the mid seventeenth century. Liberal Puritanism also produced 'the gentle tolerance of Lord Brooke, the revolutionary logic of Roger Williams, the democratic radicalism of John Lilburne, the mystical communism of Gerard Winstanley, the enthusiastic idealism of

Sir Henry Vane.'[241] And there were more systematic thinkers, like Hugo Grotius before him, and John Locke after him. Why focus on Milton?

In the first place, because he commands attention. He made his life iconic, by flirting with the idea of his prophetic calling, by performing intellectual and artistic virtuousity. And of course his eloquence, in poetry and prose, remains compelling. Some say that he was not an original thinker, that he echoed others' ideas, and was part of a general intellectual movement, a shared vision. There's some truth in this, yet there is something very distinctive about the passionate seriousness with which he tries to hammer his thoughts into unity (to borrow a nice phrase from Yeats). There is something unique about the boldness with which he attacks religious traditionalism, and imagines a post-institutional future for Christianity. I am not quite saying that his soul was like a star and dwelt apart, but there is something about his writing that sets it apart, that keeps it audible.

How have critics reacted to his theological radicalism? With two different forms of disdain. The first begins with Johnson's Tory Anglican disdain: how could this 'sect of one' have anything useful to teach the Christian church? His religious identity is disturbingly blank, says Johnson:

> We know rather what he was not, than what he was. He was not of the church of Rome; he was not of the church of England. To be of no church is dangerous. Religion, of which the rewards are distant, and which is animated only by Faith and Hope, will glide by degrees out of the mind, unless it be invigorated and re-impressed by external ordinances, by stated calls to worship, and the salutary influence of example.[242]

And for Johnson his theology is fully tainted by his politics:

> [His] republicanism was, I am afraid, founded in an envious hatred of greatness, and a sullen desire of independence; in petulance, impatient

---

241 Burton 1942, p. 332.
242 Samuel Johnson, 'Lives of the Poets', in Johnson, *Prose and Poetry*, selected by Mona Wilson, London: Rupert Hart-Davis, 1950, p. 828.

of controul, and pride disdainful of superiority. He hated monarchs in the state, and prelates in the church; for he hated all whom he was required to obey. It is to be suspected that his predominant desire was to destroy rather than establish, and that he felt not so much the love of liberty as repugnance to authority'.[243]

A generation or so after Johnson, a new sort of disdain took root. Most of the Romantics praised him to the skies, in various confused ways, but the most influential Romantic critic was actually Keats, who recoiled with horror at his religious commitment. It was Milton he was thinking of when he condemned poetry that has a 'palpable design on us'. (Keats' rapt praise for Shakespeare's 'negative capability' is surely the most influential move in all of modern literary criticism: it establishes a quasi-theology, in which literature attains the highest value by its disavowal of an ideological agenda. The quasi-theology inhabits Modernism too: Pound and Yeats basically agree with Keats.)

Some critics (often Catholics) have deepened the Johnsonian strain of disdain, denying that he was a Christian at all. Belloc calls *De Doctrina* 'his secret attack on religion'.[244] It was here, he tells us with horror, that Milton 'renounced the Creed'.[245] Belloc subtly conflates the Nicene Creed with the faith itself. His secret work was

a landmark in the break-up of European religion. It shows on the surface of English Protestantism like the first thin crack one finds on the ice of a frozen pond, which will soon grow to a broad fissure, until the general ruin of the whole surface in the full thaw . . . It was a blow struck at the very root of that which is above all other doctrines the essential doctrine of a Christian man – that Jesus is God: and therefore went on to demolish the rest of that on which our culture still precariously reposes.[246]

---

243   Ibid., p. 829.
244   Belloc 1935, p. 82.
245   Ibid., p. 287.
246   Ibid., p. 291–2.

T. S. Eliot agrees that Milton's theological liberalism is a thing of horror, yet he half-hides his Catholic disdain behind some specially concocted literary theory which blames Milton for something called a 'dissociation of sensibility', which apparently occurred at this time. What he really wants to say, it seems to me, is that Milton's thought helped to pull down a sacramental Catholic view of the world: Belloc is a more honest, less pretentious Catholic critic.

The Keatsian disdain is intensified by Empson, who brings a Dawkins-like hatred of religion, as if any conception of divine authority is mental fascism. The virtue of *Paradise Lost*, he says, is that it unwittingly 'makes God so bad', alerting us to the evil of Christianity.[247]

What about C. S. Lewis: surely he has no disdain for Milton's Christianity? He told critics with secularizing agendas: 'Milton's thought, when purged of its theology, does not exist.'[248] Yes, but Lewis wants to purge his theology of its radicalism, preferring to focus on *Paradise Lost*, whose core theology 'all Christendom in all lands or ages can accept.'[249] He is essentially of Johnson's party: Milton the poet is great; Milton the thinker is an embarrassment to good Christians.

The Johnsonian and the Keatsian strains of disdain are combined by Rowse. At the beginning of his study of Milton he bluntly states his own preference for aestheticism over Christianity, and yet later on he takes a Johnsonian line on Milton's brand of faith: he failed to see that ordinary people need old-fashioned religion: he was guilty of 'generalizing from his own self-sufficiency to ordinary simpletons who needed such guides to keep them on the rails.'[250] This sounds offensive, but Rowse is actually voicing what is probably the critical orthodoxy: religion is intellectually and aesthetically backward, but those who are religious should at least be conservatively so, for conservative religion has social utility, and a certain aesthetic grandeur.

---

247   William Empson, *Milton's God*, London: Chatto and Windus 1961, p. 275.
248   Lewis 1960, p. 65.
249   Ibid., p. 92.
250   Rowse 1977, p. 208.

A. N. Wilson seems to offer a muted version of Rowse's high-camp disdain. Though Milton believed in an austere Old Testament God, '[n]othing in his poems, although he was technically a Christian of sorts, suggests the very slightest warmth of feeling about the person of Christ.'[251] For Wilson he is more of a neo-classical republican deist, whose *deus ex machina* brings liberty.

Wilson's judgement seems influenced by Christopher Hill, who implies that he was one of the first deists, those Protestants who wanted to convert Christianity into a rationalist moral system, free of supernatural baggage.

> There is in him none of the fevered search for personal salvation that we find in Vaughan on the one hand, in Bunyan on the other. Milton is concerned with Christ's kingdom, the good society, rather than with personal consolations or rewards . . . Milton's virtual abandonment of the idea of sacrificial atonement, his failure to emphasise the miracles of the New Testament, including the incarnation, the resurrection, the ascension and Pentecost, all make his approach verge on the secular . . . The seventeenth century invented the new science of 'political economy': Milton's is almost a political theology.[252]

Hill adds that '[a]ll Milton's most passionate feelings about politics and religion were negative – . . . [in the sense of] wishing to hinder hindrances to human freedom, especially intellectual freedom.'[253] It sounds from this as if he was a sort of post-Christian, whose real concern was with creating a secular-liberal state, yet he did not quite dare to admit his abandonment of the faith, even to himself. Tom Paulin has made a similar case, presenting his religion as little more than a cover for his revolutionary republicanism.

Hill's is probably the majority late-twentieth-century view: Milton was an eccentric Christian whose real passion was for a secular cause: the

---

251   Wilson 2002, p. 136.
252   Hill 1977, 460–1.
253   Ibid., p. 262.

progress of political liberty. Only when the secular cause failed did he awkwardly retreat back into his faith. But this faith can only loosely be called Christian.

Most critics these days simply keep their distance from the question of his religion. For example, Anna Beer praises his commitment to religious toleration in the opening and closing pages of her recent biography, but does not suggest that he made any contribution to Christian thought. This should not particularly surprise us. Today's literary critics will naturally treat Milton from a secular literary perspective; it is not for them to either praise or blame his theological distinctiveness, or to say whether it really counts as Christian. That is for theologians to pass comment on.

In my theological opinion, Milton ought to be celebrated as England's greatest religious thinker, and one of the few truly great Protestants.

First of all, he was not a deist, one who retreats into rationalist semi-agnosticism. He valued liberty, and reason, as the deists did, and suspected religious authorities, in fact even more intensely than most of the desists did (many were good Anglicans), but it is absurd to think that he wanted to purge Christianity of its supernatural, revealed elements. On the contrary, he consistently sought to convey the absolute authority and the eschatological victory of the God who is revealed in Jesus Christ. He sought to convey the power of God's Word over all demonic opposition, and the need for faith in this. And some of his sonnets show a deep personal faith – yes, its expression is restrained, stoic, but that is fair enough. The theme is often trust. And, as we saw in relation to the epics, he teaches the need for something more than a vague faith in historical progress: we need to believe in God's cosmic miracle, his righting of life. If we only had his prose, critics might be semi-excused for trying to argue that his motivation was secular-political, and that he affected to be more religious than he was. It seems to me that questioning of his Christian identity can only come from a rigid ideological agenda, whether religious (he was not a real Christian like me) or secular (he was a secular radical like me).

So he was a Christian. But what are my grounds for calling him an important Christian thinker, rather than an inconsequential eccentric, as most suppose? It seems to me that he took the logic of Protestantism to a new level. What on earth is 'the logic of Protestantism'? A determination that the Gospel should be free of worldly authoritarianism. Of course Luther, Zwingli and Calvin primarily want to free the Gospel from the Roman Catholic Church. But this brings new authoritarian dangers. Luther offers the state great power over the church, which is risky, and Zwingli and Calvin enable a new sort of authoritative church that takes control of politics. England essentially followed Luther's model: a strong state church ejected Rome. What Milton and his fellow Puritans realized is that the national church that resulted was only half free from the logic of Rome. There was a still a grand institution claiming authority over the Gospel, claiming the right to impose uniformity. The main opposition movement, Calvinism, wanted to replace this with another style of strong religious institution. What Milton realized, and most Puritans did not, was that it was necessary to rethink the Constantinian revolution that had empowered the Christian church. Long before most of his fellow countrymen could grasp the concept, he was arguing for disestablishment.

Milton's revolutionary insight was that a central institution regulating Christianity was unnecessary – indeed it stood in the way of a renewal of Christian faith. Christianity ought to ally itself with freedom. This was taking Luther's vision to a new stage. Luther had argued that the ruler must step in and regulate Christian culture, by means of a state church. He took it for granted that there had to be religious uniformity. For Milton, Protestantism had to move beyond the itch for uniformity. As he said in *Areopagitica*, which might actually be his most important theological work, we require 'the reforming of Reformation itself'.[254] We need to move beyond the rigid systems of Zwingli and Calvin, which are insufficiently open to liberty. But how could the state cohere, except by imposing religious uniformity? By creating a new sort of religious culture, of liberal Protestantism. In such a culture, there is no official religious institution; there is a free market of churches. The state's role, in relation to religion, is to stop a monopoly emerging. The great frustration of his life was that Cromwell's regime never quite dared to grasp this

---

254   Ibid., p. 553.

nettle, and dismantle the established church, and its scaffolding of tithes. As we saw, the principle of the separation of church and state became increasingly important to him. He re-imagined England as essentially liberty-loving; he said that this idea was more fundamental to it than its constitutional reality, of bishops and king.

The state must be secular. In this context 'secular' does not mean anti-religious, or even neutral. It means actively opposed to religious institutions wielding power. And for Milton the state must be *Protestant* in order to be secular. It must explicitly affirm the historical narrative in which reactionary Catholicism is rejected – and it must reject Calvinism too, for this carries a new theocratic itch (whose recent expression is the religious right in America). So liberal Protestantism is the necessary basis for political progress.

But Milton's vision does not just relate to theories of the liberal Protestant state. He saw that this political revolution had to be accompanied by a religious one, by a new understanding of Christianity. His real radicalism is the deconstruction of 'orthodoxy'. He saw, more clearly than any thinker that I know of, that the concept of orthodoxy is a tool of ecclesiastical authoritarianism. With quiet stubborn courage, he stood back from the established church, and also from its main opposition movement, in order to ask what Christianity was meant to be. And he prioritised the theme of liberty – Paul's great insight that God was sick of legalism, of rules. This had been revived by Luther, of course, but subsequent reformers had let it be obscured. Luther himself had only partially stayed true to his own insight: he saw the need for the strict policing of certain doctrines, most notably the eucharist. Milton was astonishingly liberal: let each Christian decide what is the core of Christian faith, let each decide what forms of prayer and ritual seem appropriate. This extreme liberalism leads most critics to assume that he secretly tended to scepticism. If he was a real Christian then surely he would insist on shared public rules about what counts as Christian belief and practice. His style of religion will lead to agnosticism, atheism, they add. One can only respond that Milton's anti-institutionalism did not make him an agnostic or atheist. Instead it spurred him into creating great pieces of Christian culture.

But does his scepticism towards organized religion not leave a big hole in his religious vision? What is his positive vision of Christian culture? As we saw in *De Doctrina*, he affirms the 'congregational' ideal, of lots of little 'free' churches doing their own thing. To a large extent he is imagining America's religious culture (and also Britain's alternative religious culture, of Dissent). But there is another component to his positive vision, that we noted in one of his early tracts, *The Reason of Church Government*. He wants Christianity to spill over into mainstream culture, what we now call secular culture. He wants it to be the main content of plays and songs and public festivals, 'the arts'. And of course his own authorship models this: here, in this poetry, is an example of how Christianity might be post-ecclesially expressed. Christianity can break out of church and *be culture*. It sounds corny to say that this idea is still before its time, but it is.

So his religious vision could be summed up as 'ultra-Protestant', in that it revives Luther's early Pauline radicalism in a way that mainstream Protestantism cannot condone. There is an affinity with various sectarian radicals – yet such radicals, as we saw in relation to the Quakers, lacked his political sophistication, his belief in the need for a strong liberal state. And his vision is echoed by some of the awkwardest modern religious thinkers: Kierkegaard, Tolstoy, early Barth and late Bonhoeffer. But it seems to me that he is actually more consistent than any of these in his 'post-ecclesial' radicalism.

What happened to Milton's vision? One half of it flourished, the other has struggled to get off the ground. His belief in the separation of church and state was half-vindicated in England after his death, with the rise of the Whigs – of course the Church was not disestablished but its potential for reaction was restrained. And his vision more fully triumphed across the Atlantic. Milton was lauded by many of the Founding Fathers, and in 1846, R. W. Griswold declared: 'Milton is more emphatically *American* than any other author who has lived in the United States.'[255] And of course his work continued to inspire the struggle for greater liberalism in Britain too.

---

255   Quoted in Lewalski 2000, p. 545.

But what of the religious side of his vision – the idea that Christianity can flourish away from authoritative churches, that it must undergo a sort of anarchic revolution in order to renew its appeal to modernity? This vision had some influence on the liberal Protestantism of Britain and America over the next two centuries, but failed to shift the paradigm. The strongest forms of Protestantism remained essentially Calvinist: for example Wesley's movement entailed a reaction against liberalism. And during the twentieth century, Protestantism's anti-liberal tendency intensified, to the point that 'liberal Protestantism' is seen by most theologians as deeply dated. For reasons whose analysis lies beyond the scope of this book, we seem to live in age in which religious identity defines itself against secular liberalism rather than tries to accept it, work within it. Can this change? Yes, and I believe that Milton's vision is an important resource for changing it. He can point us beyond the sterile opposition of 'religious' and 'secular' that thwarts fresh thought about the meaning of Christianity.

Let me finish with a last swipe at the lit-crit consensus. Shakespeare's famous superiority to Milton is at least questionable. When I think about Shakespeare in relation to Milton, he feels a bit like Hollywood – great entertainment, at its best: thrilling stuff, wise and funny and life-enhancing, but not absolutely serious. Absolute seriousness means engagement in the debates about political and religious meaning, in renewing the myths the culture lives by. Yes, of course Shakespeare is interested in 'meaning'. But the detachment is chilly. His hands are too clean. And does not Rowse protest too much about Shakespeare's manliness? Is there not something rather effete about confining oneself to playhouses and speaking only through their magic ghosts? Is there not a sort of camp cowardice in Shakespeare's decision to step back from the Protestant revolution and revert to a neo-pagan thought-world? Is there not something manlier, braver, and simply more honestly human about daring to work out what you think, and putting eloquence in the service of telling it straight?

Index